Lessons for the Young
ECONOMIST

Teacher's Manual

Lessons for the Young
ECONOMIST

Teacher's Manual

ROBERT P. MURPHY

For information write the Ludwig von Mises Institute
518 West Magnolia Avenue, Auburn, Alabama 36832. Mises.org

ISBN: 978-1-61016-204-3

Contents

PART I: FOUNDATIONS

PART II: CAPITALISM: THE MARKET ECONOMY

PART III: SOCIALISM: THE COMMAND ECONOMY

PART IV: INTERVENTIONISM: THE MIXED ECONOMY

Preface

This is the Teacher's Manual to accompany the student text, *Lessons for the Young Economist*, published by the Ludwig von Mises Institute. The student text is available for free online, or it can be purchased as a physical book, at this web address: **http://mises.org/resources/5706/Lessons-for-the-Young-Economist**. The student text was designed with junior high students in mind, but it is applicable for younger, precocious students, and also even for adults who never got a solid grounding in free-market economic principles.

This Manual is intended to guide the teacher through the course, giving the broader context of the material in the student text, as well as offering suggested test questions and further activities. It can be used by classroom teachers, but is also ideally suited to homeschooling instruction by parents who may not be confident in their own economics knowledge.

Here's how the Manual works: First, before introducing a particular chapter (or Lesson), the teacher needs to read it in the student text. Then, the teacher should read the accompanying material in the Manual. For each section of each chapter, the Manual may give the historical context, clarify the relationship between what the student is learning from the text compared to a typical college textbook, warn about possible confusions the student may encounter, give links for the teacher's own edification (not necessarily to be assigned to the student), and so forth.

After walking through the main body of the student text in a given chapter, the Manual then provides thorough answers to the Study Questions found at the back of each Lesson. The Manual then lists optional supplemental materials, which are free online videos, audio lectures, and readings, along with instructions as to their level of difficulty and relevance, helping the teacher determine which (if any) to assign.

Next the Manual will list one or more Suggested Activities, which are applied ways to illustrate the concepts from the chapter. Some of the activities will be suitable for classroom use, while others will be more relevant for homeschooling families where the teacher and student will be out in the "real world" together on a regular basis.

Finally, each chapter of the Manual ends with a sample test, which can be printed out (if the teacher is using a PDF version) or copied (if using a physical book). The physical version of the Teacher's Manual also contains an answer key to the sample tests, while the online PDF version only has the tests. (This is to make it harder for students to look up the answers beforehand.)

The sample tests for each chapter don't follow a set format. Sometimes there are true/false, sometimes multiple choice, sometimes fill-in-the-blank, and there are also many short answer questions. The idea is to give the teacher samples of various styles, to help in the creation of a teacher's own tests based on the material.

Within the answer key, for each short answer question, the Manual will give a sample "full credit" answer. The point here is to show what a "model" answer would look like; the teacher will have to decide what is actually worth full credit, because a fair threshold might be far lower than what the Manual shows as a great answer. The Manual will often (but not always) also list "partial" and "no credit" answers, to help the teacher understand the central concept of the question. Sometimes a "no credit" answer will actually be a true statement, but it will completely miss what the question is trying to elicit, showing that the student didn't grasp that section of the text.

In addition to the student text and Teacher's Manual, the Mises Institute also plans on holding recurring offerings of Robert Murphy's online Mises Academy class, covering the main sections of the book. The current course listing is available at: **http://academy.mises.org/**.

It is the Mises Institute's sincere hope that *Lessons for the Young Economist* and this accompanying Teacher's Manual foster a convenient introduction for young people to the fascinating and vital subject of free-market economic principles. Both classroom and homeschool instructors are encouraged to relay their feedback (**Murphy@mises.com**) on how they are using the materials, and ways to improve future editions.

Part I

FOUNDATIONS

Thinking Like an Economist

Although most economists would endorse the themes of the material in Part I: Foundations, there are several areas where the views in the student textbook differ from what is taught in a standard text. We will point these differences out to you as we work through the book, and explain the reasons for the disagreement.

One of the biggest differences is the simple fact that we spend so much time on foundations in the first place. In most texts, there is an urge to "jump right into the economics." However, in this course we have adopted the admittedly old-fashioned idea that you need to lay a foundation before building a house. We hope that the approach in this course, including its emphasis on understanding the nature and scope of economics, is intuitive and commonsensical. In contrast, many of the problems in higher economics—as practiced at the most prestigious universities—can be traced precisely to its failure to pay attention to these issues which are often derided as "philosophy" rather than economics.

As with much of the material in this course, our approach to economic foundations is based on the work of Ludwig von Mises. If you want to read more of Mises's views, you can read the first chapter of Mises's *Epistemological Problems of Economics*, available at: **http://mises.org/epofe.asp.** However, you should be warned that Mises's writing style can be difficult at first, and you also need to know that for Mises, economics is a branch of praxeology, his term for "the science of human action."

Some students will be more receptive to the material in Part I, whereas others will be impatient to "get to the actual economics." Obviously we included the material in these opening lessons because we deemed it important for a proper education. However, for students who are impatient to learn something "useful," the first two chapters can be omitted without compromising the material in subsequent lessons. But every student should at least read Lesson 3, because Lesson 4 is where the meat of the instruction begins, so it should be studied carefully.

Thinking Like an Economist

In this section we are trying to get the student excited about the subject, by explaining its relation to other disciplines. Some economists engage in what has been called "imperialism" by trying to apply economic logic to every facet of life, including an "economic analysis" of dating.

In our view, there is a danger in overpromising the benefits of economics, and that is why we have tried to place it in its proper role among other disciplines. The principles or laws that we develop in this course do apply to all situations where people face scarcity and so must make choices that involve tradeoffs. However, just because a particular economic "tool" applies doesn't mean that it is necessarily *useful*.

For an analogy, a physicist could make plenty of true statements about the high school prom, involving conservation of energy, the rotational inertia of dancing couples, and so forth. But it would be ridiculous for physicists to start lecturing parents and school administrators on the results obtained from their study of the "physics of proms."

In the same light, in this course we focus on traditional topics of economic analysis. We think it's far more important to educate students on matters such as minimum wage laws and inflation, rather than racier (and perhaps more exciting) topics that you will see covered by popular economics books on the shelves at Barnes & Noble. Even so, if your student is eager for a completely unexpected application of the tools being developed during the course, you can urge him or her to be patient for the topic of drug prohibition covered in Lesson 20. In that chapter, many students will be surprised by how easily they can "make sense" of the stylized facts concerning black markets in drugs, using the apparently mundane tools that they will have learned by that point.

Is Economics a Science?

In this section we adopt a definitely *minority* viewpoint, so you should be aware of the controversy. Most economists would agree with our take that economics is a science. However, many (perhaps most) economists would say that what makes economics a science is its ultimate reliance on *falsifiable predictions*.

The economists who adopt this view are (whether they know it or not) following in the tradition crystallized by Milton Friedman in his famous essays on what is called "positive economics." If you want to learn more about this controversy, you should first read the essays in the Supplemental Materials for Lessons 1 and 2, and then for further discussion you should listen to philosopher Roderick Long's discussion of Friedman versus Mises at **http://mises.org/media/4006.**

In a nutshell, the economists who follow Friedman adopt the view of Karl Popper, who argued that in order for a statement to be scientific, it had to be falsifiable. In other words, it had to be at least possible in principle for the facts to turn out a certain way, in order to render the statement false. If this were not possible, then (according to Popperians and those economists who endorsed Friedman's views on this matter) the statement would not be scientific at all.

It is understandable why many academics, who wish their work to be "objective" and free from personal bias, endorse the Popperian view. If one's model of the world can't be proven wrong, no matter what happens, then it seems to be a dogma or "religion."

However, Ludwig von Mises and those who follow his views on this issue of the nature of economics, do not believe economic theory is composed of testable propositions. This recognition doesn't therefore prove that economics is a mere dogma; it rather (according to Misesians) shows that the Popperian insistence on falsifiability is a bad criterion for science.

This is a deep philosophical controversy and your student can skim through the material if it is too difficult. Just be aware that standard textbooks would say that yes economics is a science, but only because it relies on testable predictions. Ironically, the textbook will then go on to teach principles—such as "People respond to incentives" and "All choices involve trade-offs"—which are not testable! This was Mises's whole point, and it is the reason we have adopted his approach for this course. It is a simple confusion to try to model economics on physics or chemistry, and assume that in order to be scientific, economics must consist of testable or falsifiable predictions.

As far as distinguishing economic science from other human inventions that truly *are* unscientific—perhaps astrological "forecasts" as reported in newspapers—we can simply ask the reader whether he or she has a better understanding of the world, after learning the material in this course. Geometry too is "non-falsifiable" in the sense of Karl Popper, but it is not merely a collection of arbitrary conventions and definitions. There is a very real sense in which students understand the real world better, after they have learned the basics of geometry. We hope the same will be true after learning basic economics.

The Scope and Boundaries of Economic Science

The material in this section is mostly offered for the benefit of those students who like to be very organized and have a solid understanding of what it is that they are about to begin studying. It's very important for the student to realize that economics is not simply the study of business or money, even though economics obviously does include these concepts.

If we are telling the student what economics *is not*, then we ought to follow up by saying what it *is*. For the purposes of this course, it is accurate enough to say that economics is the study of exchanges.

Most economists would probably have no objection to defining economics as the study of exchanges, but some of them would take issue with our discussion of the hypothetical "economic man." In many textbooks and even popular expositions of economics, the authors will say that economists must construct models of people "as if" they were (a) very selfish and (b) capable of solving complicated mathematical problems without ever making a mistake.

We reject that approach in this course. This difference goes back to the more fundamental disagreement over the nature of economics. Since we believe basic economic theory consists of a (non-testable) way of viewing the world, we can't anchor it to (false) assumptions about human motivations and computational abilities.

In contrast, for those economists who think economics is a collection of testable predictions, then there is nothing wrong in making "simplifying assumptions" in order to yield crisp predictions. They can justify their approach with analogies to physics, where (for example) the scientist can make general predictions about the path of a baseball without dealing with complications such as the gravitational pull of a nearby butterfly.

For our purposes, it is enough that the student recognizes that the principles or laws of economics *as we develop them in this course* are not dependent on a particular view of man as being an "egoist," and they do not assume that people are superhuman calculators. On the one hand, this allows our principles to be true for all people, but on the other we can only make general statements about tendencies, rather than precise predictions which can then be measured experimentally.

Why Study Economics?

In this final section, we try to motivate the student to work through the material in the coming lessons, some of which will be difficult. If necessary, you should help your student pace him or herself by warning that the true payoff may not become apparent until Part III of the course. At that point, the tools that we develop for understanding a market economy can be used to explain why *deviations* from a market economy lead to disastrous outcomes. Beyond the horrors described in Part III, the material in Part IV should also prove very interesting to students, as it will explain such "facts of life" as unemployment and the business cycle, and show that they are largely the result of government intervention.

However, in order for the student to fully appreciate these later applications, he or she must first master the principles. We encourage you to force impatient students through the material in Part II before jumping into the "fun" material later in the book.

If you want to pursue additional reading on the role of economics in society—and in particular the duty of the average citizen to learn basic economics—you should read Part Seven of Mises's masterpiece, *Human Action*, available at **http://mises. org/Books/HumanActionScholars.pdf.**

• •

STUDY QUESTIONS

1. Can economics make you rich?

In the text we have taken the position that basic economics *per se* won't guarantee financial success, but that being ignorant of basic economics is a good way to ensure failure. An analogy might be the study of geometry and building a bridge that can support traffic—studying geometry isn't enough, but it's definitely necessary.

More generally, economists fall into two camps on this question. The purists insist that even a trained economist doesn't have the ability to, say, predict stock price movements more accurately than hedge fund managers. On the other hand, many economists think that investors can outperform their peers—especially in times characterized by heavy government intervention—if they are guided by sound economics. For example, several economists and investment advisors warned of the housing bubble in the early and mid-2000s while there was still time to "get out," and they credited the business cycle theory we will explain in Lesson 23 as their inspiration.

2. Is economics a science? Why or why not?

Of course the text's answer is "yes," so long as the student understands that economics is not the same type of science as physics or chemistry. However, the important point is to understand the issue of logical versus empirical disciplines; we will discuss this more in Lesson 2. If a particular student wants to reserve the term *science* for those intellectual enterprises that rely on falsifiable theories and experimental tests, then economics is not a science. But to concede this point doesn't mean economics is arbitrary or has nothing to do with the real world; mathematics doesn't rely on experiments either, and so it too would be "unscientific" using this criterion.

3. Does scarcity affect everyone?

Yes. The important point here is that scarcity is not the same thing as poverty. We can imagine a world of fantastic material wealth, where no one goes hungry or even gets sick. But it would be difficult to even imagine a world without scarcity, in which someone's actions didn't come with costs. If nothing else, people would still have only a limited number of hours per day in which to act. Even immortals with superfast spaceships would still have to decide (say) whether to visit Galaxy A first or Galaxy B.

4. Do the laws of economics still work inside a maximum security prison?

Yes, the laws of economics (as developed in this course) do not rest on particular assumptions. They are universal, as are the laws of physics. However, in certain settings it might be difficult to apply or illustrate a particular economic law. For example, the principles we develop for the Robinson Crusoe world (in Lesson 4) apply to each person in a maximum security prison, but because the environment is so different, it might be hard to "see" certain effects. It's still true that the prisoners could (in principle) enhance their productive output by saving and investing resources, but if the guards (or other prisoners) would take anything they were working on, it would be pointless for them to do so.

5. *Isn't it just as important for the average person to understand particle physics, since much of the funding for this research comes from government grants?

This is a difficult question because the student could take the answer in several directions. We would say the answer is "no,"

---

*An asterisk indicates a more challenging question.

because government funding for particle physics would never constitute the same impact on an economy as other government programs that are based on faulty economic views. Also, even a basic education in economics (such as the one provided in this course) is enough to demonstrate the absurdity behind most of the economic justifications for various government policies. In contrast, one would need to do much more research to be able to decide how much physicists were exaggerating the benefits of bigger government budgets for their pet projects.

Supplemental Materials

- Gene Callahan, *Economics for Real People* available at **http://mises.org/resources/2031**, Chapter 1 and Appendix A.

> Callahan's book was commissioned and published by the Mises Institute (the producers of this course). It is intended as an introduction to Austrian economics, which is the school of thought associated with Ludwig von Mises. Callahan's book, as well as the Lew Rockwell essay listed below, provide an explanation for the term "Austrian" and explain the relationship of the Austrian School to others, such as the Keynesian or Chicago School. For this course, the student doesn't need to learn the particulars of Austrian economics vs. other types of schools. But in the Supplemental Materials, these terms unavoidably come up and so the student will need to know what they mean.

> We should make it clear that most of the lessons in this course do not depend on "Austrian" economics per se; any professional economist who has an affinity for free markets would endorse or at least sympathize with the approach. The only chapters that owe an explicit debt to the Austrian School are Lessons 15 and 23, because they rely on the particular theories of Ludwig von Mises, the dean of the Austrian School in the twentieth century.

- Robert Murphy, "The Core of What Economics Teaches," video available at **http://mises.org/MediaPlayer. aspx?Id=4988**

> Despite the official title of the lecture, this talk was intended to give high school students a sample of the insights that economics can give in unexpected settings. It is self-explanatory.

- Lew Rockwell, "Why Austrian Economics Matters," available at **http://mises.org/etexts/why_ae.asp**

  As we mentioned above, the course set out here (in *Lessons for the Young Economist*) is not about Austrian economics. It is a general introduction to economic principles, coming from a free-market perspective. However, everyone who worked on the course's development has an affinity for the Austrian School, and this has undoubtedly influenced the presentation of the material. In his essay, Lew Rockwell—the founder of the Mises Institute—explains why a growing number of academics and laypeople keep returning to the ideas of a school of economic thinking that at one time was considered a closed chapter in history.

- Nassau Senior, "An Introductory Lecture on Political Economy," available at **http://mises.org/books/selected_writings_senior. pdf.**

  Nassau Senior was a classical economist, meaning that he wrote before the so-called Marginalist (or Subjectivist) Revolution of 1871. (For an explanation see Joe Salerno's lecture at **http://mises.org/media/4344**). We have included the lecture from Senior mainly to give the interested student a taste of what economics (or "political economy") was like before the hyper-mathematization of the twentieth century.

  We emphasize that a modern economist would not necessarily endorse everything Senior writes, just as a modern political theorist wouldn't agree with everything in Aristotle's works. For example, Senior assumes the task of economics is to understand the accumulation of material wealth, whereas modern economics no longer focuses on that as its primary function. Some students might find Senior's work too difficult at this early stage, when they have just been introduced to modern economic principles as developed in this course. You will have to decide whether the possible confusion outweighs the benefit of seeing a historical document.

SUGGESTED ACTIVITIES

Discuss with the student the various things that every "well-rounded" young adult should have studied. For example, the list might include arithmetic and algebra (but not necessarily calculus), famous works of literature, key portions of world history, the major events in the history of physics, and so on. The purpose of the activity isn't so much to come up with the list, but to discuss what factors put something on the list (or keep it off). After you have come up with a set of criteria for what puts something on the list (or keeps it off), see if basic economic principles should make the cut.

True or False on Basic Ideas:

Write true if the statement is true or write false if the statement is false.

1. _____ The economic perspective is the most important one in all situations involving people.

2. _____ Economics is important only if you're going to become a businessperson.

3. _____ At its core, economic theory cannot be tested.

4. _____ Economic "laws" aren't objective, but instead depend on the tastes of the researcher.

Matching Essential Terminology:

Write the BEST answer on each line beside its description.

Social Science   **Tradeoffs**   **Dilemma**   **Barter**

Scarcity   **Exchanges**

5. _____ The subject that economics studies.

6. _____ A situation when traders exchange goods or services directly for each other without money.

7. _____ The fact that making one choice means that other choices become unavailable.

8. _____ The fact that there are limited resources but unlimited desires.

Short Answers (4 points each):

In one to three sentences, respond to the following prompts.

9. Explain how economics is indeed a science but not in the same sense as physics or chemistry.

_____

_____

_____

_____

_____

_____

_____

_____

10. Describe a scene in which two people barter.

_____

_____

_____

_____

_____

_____

_____

_____

_____

11. Explain why even phenomenally rich men and women need to economize on their resources and choices.

_____

_____

_____

_____

_____

_____

_____

_____

_____

True or False on Basic Ideas

1. FALSE   2. FALSE

3. TRUE   4. FALSE

Matching Essential Terminology

5. Exchanges   6. Barter

7. Tradeoffs   8. Scarcity

Short Answers (4 points each):

9. Explain how economics is indeed a science but not in the same sense as physics or chemistry.

SAMPLE FULL CREDIT ANSWER

Economics is a science because there are objective laws about "how the economy works" that can be discovered and agreed upon by independent researchers. However, the way economists discover these laws is different from how physicists or chemists conduct research in their fields. Physicists and chemists can rely on experimental tests to choose one theory over another, but that's not how economists discover their laws.

SAMPLE PARTIAL CREDIT ANSWER

Economics is a science but not like physics or chemistry. In physics the scientists can perform tests, but economists can't do this.

SAMPLE NO CREDIT ANSWER

Economics studies things like money and employment, but physics studies electricity and gravity.

10. Describe a scene in which two people barter.

SAMPLE FULL CREDIT ANSWER
John has a peanut butter sandwich while Mary has a bologna sandwich. They trade at lunchtime.

SAMPLE PARTIAL CREDIT ANSWER
Two people trade without using money.

SAMPLE NO CREDIT ANSWER
John goes to the store but doesn't buy anything because he has no money.

11. Explain why even phenomenally rich men and women need to economize on their resources and choices.

SAMPLE FULL CREDIT ANSWER
Even Bill Gates can't achieve everything he can imagine. He can't go to the moon tomorrow, or give everyone in Africa a mansion. He is also limited by how many hours he has in the day, to accomplish various goals.

SAMPLE PARTIAL CREDIT ANSWER
There are some things money can't buy.

SAMPLE NO CREDIT ANSWER
No matter how rich someone is, there will always be someone richer or at least there might be in the near future.

How We Develop
Economic Principles

The material in this chapter would not be contained in standard textbooks, and indeed (as we explained in the previous chapter) many economists might not even agree with some of its themes. Naturally we will be clear in the sections below to point out these areas of disagreement.

If a particular student cannot handle abstract thought very well, Lesson 2 can safely be omitted. However, the material in this chapter is important to truly understand what we are doing when we use economics to understand the world.

Purposeful Action versus Mindless Behavior

This section emphasizes the crucial distinction between purposeful action and mindless behavior. It's important for the student to learn that the economist must "get inside the head"—or more accurately, inside the *mind*—of the people acting in a market.

Superficially, it appears that economics is about physical things—dollar bills, tractors, factories, and television sets. But economics is really about the (mental) *decisions* that people make, concerning those physical things. A human decision, or choice, is an intangible concept; it can't be weighed or otherwise measured.

The Social versus the Natural Sciences

In this section we simply reiterate the fundamental distinction between social and natural sciences. In the social sciences we (typically) must rely not only on observable, physical things but also must rely on our interpretations of other people's mental activities.

To stress the point yet again, note that "mental activities" does *not* mean "electrical activity in someone's nervous system." It is a basic confusion at the outset to think that a description of someone else's thoughts, feelings, and motivations is the same thing as a description of that person's physiological processes. Now some researchers are making great progress in showing the *connection* between physical states of the brain and, say, feelings of aggression or creative thought. We are not taking a stand on the deep philosophical issues of dualism and the mind-body problem, if you are familiar with those controversies. All we are saying is that talk of a person's mental "events" is on a different plane from talk of the operations of his or her physical brain.

The reason we stress these points is that it will shed light on the later sections, and why we argue that basic economics is a logical, deductive framework rather than a set of empirical propositions that need to be tested.

The Success of the Natural Sciences versus the Social Sciences

In this section we remind people of the difference in reputation and prestige among the various sciences. It is undeniable that the natural scientists seem much more . . . scientific . . . than the social scientists. By now it should be clear why we have spent so much time developing philosophical points that (apparently) have little to do with an introduction to economics. The techniques that lead to success and credibility in the natural sciences do not seem to work as well in the social sciences. Now we can see the role for an entirely different approach to economics, as we explain in the next section.

How We Develop Basic Economics

Finally the work of the prior sections yields the payoff, where we now can explain the development of basic economic principles or laws. We start with some basic truths or "axioms" about purposeful action and then we logically deduce implications from these self-evident (or at least non-controversial) building blocks.

The analogy with geometry is probably the best one available, because the student will be familiar with it and also because there is no denying that geometrical proofs are important truths about the "real world." In other words, people who would criticize the approach to economics adopted in this course would be hard-pressed to apply their criticisms to geometry.

If you are capable of presenting it, an actual proof of the Pythagorean Theorem might drive home the point. There are several proofs that you can survey at the Wikipedia article at **http://en.wikipedia.org/wiki/Pythagorean_theorem**. Depending on the math skills of the student in question, one proof might be easier to grasp than another. (For example, some are quite intuitive, relying on a simple rearrangement of shapes, while others rely on algebra.) The purpose of this exercise would be to drive home the point of the power of a deductive proof: Once the student really gets it and can see how the proof of the Pythagorean Theorem works, he or she would realize that it's silly to go out and "test" the theorem on various right triangles.

In addition to the Supplemental Materials, you can learn more about this approach to economic principles by watching a lecture by economist Hans Hoppe at **http://mises.org/ media/4347/Praxeology-The-Austrian-Method**. Hoppe comes from a philosophical background and has a thick accent, so some viewers may find it difficult to follow. Roderick Long discusses similar issues in a lecture discussing "a priorism and positivism in the social sciences," the audio is available at **http://mises.org/media/4017**. (A priorism and positivism are defined in Long's lecture.)

• •

STUDY QUESTIONS

1. If someone sneezes when pepper is thrown in his face, is that a purposeful action?

The answer is no, because (presumably) sneezing is a reflexive behavior. It's important for the student to realize that the distinction between purposeful action and mindless behavior is not simply the difference between human bodily movements versus items in nature. As the example of lifting a leg in the student text shows, human behavior can be classified as either purposeful action or mindless behavior, depending on the circumstances.

2. Does "purposeful action" include mistakes?

Yes, it does. Purposeful action is intentional action; it is behavior that serves a purpose to the thing doing the behaving. People try to achieve certain outcomes and fail, all the time. Yet they are still acting with purpose. In this course we do not assume that people are flawless calculators, as some textbook writers do.

3. *Are brain and mind interchangeable terms?

No, they are not. The brain is a physical organ of the body, whereas the mind is an intangible concept that obviously bears some relationship to the brain. (Note that someone can "lose his mind" without losing his brain.) To repeat, we are not ruling out particular theories of neuroscience that claim that certain mental states are caused by particular brain states. We are making the very modest point that mental states or operations (such as anxiety, happiness, long-range planning, multiplication, etc.) are different from brain states (such as firing neurons and blood flow to the left hemisphere).

4. Can we perform controlled experiments to test economic theories?

No, not in the same sense that we perform controlled experiments in (some of) the natural sciences. There is an entire field called "experimental economics," in which researchers will run experiments to test various issues that are important to some economic researchers. For example, in one experiment the subjects are grouped into pairs. The first subject is allowed to divide up (say) $10 between himself and the other person in his group. He can keep it all for himself, give $5 to the other person and to himself, etc. Now the experiments have shown that the method for determining who is first (and gets to split the money) can affect the fairness of the split. If the first person is chosen randomly, he or she tends to give a fairer split than if the first person is decided by having the two people in the group first play some type of competitive game. The theory to explain this outcome is that the first person feels as if he or she deserves more (or all) of the money if the power position is due to "merit," whereas the first person is more worried about being selfish if his or her power is due to blind chance. (If you want to pursue this topic a good summary is here: **http://en.wikipedia.org/wiki/Dictator_game**).

Yet despite the growing field of experimental economics, nonetheless the experiments conducted on human subjects are not truly controlled, the way physicists can tinker with their experiments on electrons. (At least, the physicists think their experiments are very controlled. We ultimately don't really know.) There is always a great deal of "noise" in the results of any experiment involving human subjects. Often times particular results of a strategic game will be thrown out because "that subject obviously didn't understand the rules" and so forth. Indeed, one common finding is that students who have studied economics tend to behave more selfishly in economic experiments!

5. **Would you classify Intelligent Design theory as a natural or social science?

There is no preferred answer to this question; we offer it merely to provoke thought and discussion. The distinction we have drawn in the student text between social and natural sciences rested on the typical pattern that there are no "intentions" in the natural sciences; it would be very unscientific to say that an apple fell from a tree because it was afraid of heights. On the other hand, it is perfectly reasonable and "scientific" to bring talk of motivations and thoughts into analyses of people and their actions.

Intelligent Design theory presents an interesting challenge to this traditional dichotomy between the natural and social sciences. The biologists and other "hard" scientists who vehemently oppose Intelligent Design theory argue that it is just as unscientific as explaining volcanic eruptions by reference to angry gods. On the other hand, the proponents of Intelligent Design theory say that it is just as reasonable as a homicide detective looking at a murder scene and inferring that an intelligence had been involved. No one would criticize the detective for being unscientific if he said, "This guy's dead because his wife was angry."

To repeat, there is no preferred answer to this question, it is offered merely to get the student to really think about the different approaches to exploring the world.

Supplemental Materials

- Gene Callahan, *Economics for Real People*, Chapter 2.

  This material should be self-explanatory. Callahan jumps ahead to deal with some concepts that we will cover in later lessons of this course.

- Gene Callahan, "What Is *A Priori* Science, and Why Does Economics Qualify as One?" at **http://mises.org/daily/2025**

  This is a good introduction to Mises's methodological views on economics. It is not necessary for students to know this material for the present course, but if they want to go deeper in this topic, they will need to grapple with terms such as *a priori*.

- Robert Murphy, "Mises's Non-Trivial Insight," at **http://mises.org/daily/1304**

  This article spells out from scratch the difference between the Misesian focus on human action, versus the popular tendency to model economics after physics. Often critics of Mises dismissed his attention on action as trivial, but the article argues that it was a very deep insight.

- Robert Murphy, "Psychology versus Praxeology," at **http://mises.org/daily/1351**

  This final article should help distinguish the *a priori*, deductive approach from an empirical, inductive approach. Sometimes the emphasis on social versus natural sciences confuses readers, because they know that some social scientists—such as psychologists— use experiments all the time. This article shows the difference between experimental "laws" discovered in psychology, versus deductive laws discovered in economics. (Note that *praxeology* is Mises's term for the science of human action, which is a broad field that includes economics as one of its components.)

It is not critical for the student to memorize the precise details on these deep issues. The only really important take-away lesson is that there is a large gulf between viewing objects as mindless things, versus viewing them as intentional beings. This difference goes a long way toward explaining the varying prestige and credibility enjoyed by "hard" natural scientists versus "soft" social scientists. It also helps to explain the approach we take in this course, where we don't try to "prove" basic economic principles by reference to experiments or historical statistics.

SUGGESTED ACTIVITIES

Get the student comfortable with the distinction between purposeful action versus reflexive (mindless) behavior by working with extreme examples. For example, does the sun "want" to rise in the east every morning? Does a plant "want" to gradually move its leaves toward the sunlight? Does a dog perform a trick for a treat "on purpose"? Are the zombies in movies using means to achieve ends?

Social or Natural Science:

Identify the following sciences as either social or natural.

A. Social Science   B. Natural Science

1. _____ Biology

2. _____ Economics

3. _____ Criminology

4. _____ Astronomy

Matching Essential Terminology:

Write the appropriate term on the line beside its description.

Theorem	**Oxymoron**	**Axiom**
Freudian	**Keynesian**	**Austrian**

5. _____ A school of economic thought that calls for increased government spending during times of economic decline.

6. _____ A chain of deductive reasoning to reach a conclusion from an initial set of assumptions.

7. _____ A school of economic thought that blames faulty monetary policy for the boom–bust cycle.

8. _____ A definition or assumption from which logical deductions are made.

Short Answers (4 points each):

In one to three sentences, respond to the following prompts.

9. List two examples of mindless behaviors and two examples of purposeful actions.

Mindless behavior:

_____

_____

_____

_____

Mindless behavior:

_____

_____

_____

_____

Purposeful action:

_____

_____

_____

_____

Purposeful action:

_____

_____

_____

_____

10. Explain why the "scientific method" simply won't do well in the realm of social science.

_____

_____

_____

_____

_____

_____

_____

_____

_____

_____

_____

_____

11. Explain how economists derive economic principles or laws.

_____

_____

_____

_____

_____

_____

_____

_____

_____

_____

_____

_____

_____

_____

Social or Natural Science:

A. Social Science   B. Natural Science

1. B   2. A   3. A   4. B

Matching Essential Terminology:

5. Keynesian   6. Theorem

7. Austrian   8. Axiom

Short Answers (4 points each):

9. List two examples of mindless behaviors and two examples of purposeful actions.

Mindless behavior:

FULL CREDIT EXAMPLES
Man sneezing because of pepper or allergies, someone flinching when a car backfires, a woman shivering because it's cold.

PARTIAL CREDIT EXAMPLES
(because too vague to determine if student understands the distinction): Man yelling during a dream, a bee pollinating a flower, someone going to the bathroom.

NO CREDIT EXAMPLES
A man buying a lotto ticket, a woman lighting a cigarette, a boy putting the wrong answer on a math test.

Purposeful action:

FULL CREDIT EXAMPLES
Man adding pepper to his soup, a soldier running after throwing a grenade, a woman buying a coat because it's cold.

PARTIAL CREDIT EXAMPLES
(because too vague to determine if student understands the distinction): Man yelling during a dream, a bee pollinating a flower, someone going to the bathroom.

NO CREDIT EXAMPLES
Man running a fever to fight an infection, man sneezing because of pepper, a woman's stomach rumbling.

10. Explain why the "scientific method" simply won't do well in the realm of social science.

SAMPLE FULL CREDIT ANSWER
The social sciences study people, and so the very "facts" of the social sciences involve people's minds. The natural sciences study mindless particles and can use repeatable experiments, changing one variable at a time, to test which theories are better or worse. Yet there are no controlled experiments in the social sciences, because the people have minds of their own so that we can't ever replicate the same conditions for a new "test."

SAMPLE PARTIAL CREDIT ANSWER
Social sciences study people, and so they can't use experiments.

SAMPLE NO CREDIT ANSWER
Social scientists have not helped governments as much as physicists have.

11. Explain how economists derive economic principles or laws.

SAMPLE FULL CREDIT ANSWER

The economist develops principles the same way that mathematicians prove theorems in geometry. The economist starts out with the observation or assumption that people have conscious goals, and then logically deduces implications from that fact.

SAMPLE PARTIAL CREDIT ANSWER

The economist knows what it's like to be living in an economy, so he can understand what motivates other people too.

SAMPLE NO CREDIT ANSWER

The economist observes how people behave in the economy and then comes up with general principles to explain what he sees.

Economic Concepts Implied By Action

Introduction

I n Lesson 3 we illustrate the payoff of our attention to apparently philosophical concerns in the previous chapter. The general concepts we develop here would be ones endorsed by most professional economists, and yet (as we'll see) they are all logical implications of the fact that humans act purposefully. If a student is perplexed as to why we spent so much time in Lesson 2 on the distinction between purposeful action and mindless behavior, the answer is that purposeful action provides a proper foundation for the basic principles shared by all modern economists—even if those economists themselves don't know it!

Only Individuals Act

To say that every action requires an actor seems simple enough, but it carries surprising implications. Much of the talk in political analysis falls into the pitfall of assuming that collectives can act, rather than focusing on the individual actions that make up the combined effect.

It's important to stress that this methodological focus on the individual doesn't take a stand on whether people are "atomistic" or "social." If a crowd gets riled up by a demagogue and does something that none of the individuals would do in isolation, that fact of "crowd psychology" is perfectly consistent with what we are saying in this section. The important point is that a "crowd" per se doesn't do anything; it's always the people in the crowd who make conscious decisions.

For the present course, this emphasis on individual analysis won't seem to have profound implications. But at higher levels of theory, the difference in focusing on "micro" versus "macro" can be quite serious. For example, Keynesian economists diagnose recessions as shortfalls in aggregate spending, and this leads them to certain recommendations. Austrian economists try to trace their analysis of large "macro" events back to individual decisions. This difference in approach partly explains the diametrically opposed policy recommendations that Keynesians and Austrians give in the midst of a recession. (The Austrian view of recessions is laid out in Lesson 23.)

Individuals Have Preferences

In this section we introduce the concept of individual preferences. This is the point at which standard textbooks would normally begin the analysis. The groundwork up until now has laid the foundation for this point. Our approach will hopefully give the student a better understanding of how economics actually works, by starting at an earlier stage rather than jumping right into a discussion of preferences.

Preferences Are Subjective

This section deals with the subjectivity of preferences, which is one of the most misunderstood components of modern economics. As the text stresses, economists are *not* adopting ethical or moral relativism. There is nothing "uneconomical" in someone condemning smoking as immoral; the point is that if economists want to explain the price of tobacco, they obviously have to acknowledge the fact that many people prefer to spend their money on cigarettes versus broccoli.

We did not bring it up for fear of overloading some students, but the modern emphasis on subjective preferences actually represents a revolution in economic theory. In classical economics—developed by people such as Adam Smith—economists endorsed variations of the labor theory of value. This was an objective (not subjective) approach to explaining market prices. The modern, subjectivist value theory approach (which we use in this course) is totally different from the classical conception. For a good introduction to this revolution in economic thought, listen to Joe Salerno's lecture here: **http://mises.org/media/1463.**

Preferences Are a Ranking, Not a Measurement Using Numbers

As with much of the material in these opening chapters, the student may not understand why we are spending so much time on apparently pedantic quibbles. Rest assured, the emphasis on preferences being a *ranking*, not a measurement, will make more sense in Lesson 6 when we explain the formation of barter prices. If the student gets the basic idea down now, it will be easier for him or her to follow the discussion later.

As the "An Alternate View" box explains, high-level mainstream economics programs try to have it both ways on this issue. On the one hand, incoming doctoral candidates will learn that modern economic theory is based on preference rankings. (So far this agrees with the approach in this course.) But then after some mathematical fancy footwork, most practicing economists begin using "utility functions" that measure people's satisfaction or happiness. Although the mathematical footwork is correct, even so we think that most practicing economists forget the lessons from their early schooling, and do their research assuming that people's subjective preferences can be captured quantitatively by a utility function.

For the student who won't take further courses in economics, this tangent can safely be ignored. We are mentioning the mainstream use of utility functions solely to help advanced students relate other textbook presentations to what they are learning in this course.

Different Individuals' Preferences Can't Be Combined

In this final section we draw another implication, that preferences from different people can't be combined. We used the popular example of taking a dollar from a rich man and giving it to a poor man to motivate the idea, but the lesson applies to much of the standard discussions concerning social policies. Even many economists discuss ways of increasing "social welfare" when the foundation for such a concept is dubious. It is true that high-level economic theory can come up with a rationale for such language, but in practice many economists—let alone people outside the profession—revert to the fallacy that we can add up everybody's level of happiness and then try to maximize this number.

● ●

STUDY QUESTIONS

1. Why is it questionable to say, "Germany attacked France"?

It's inaccurate because what the statement really means is that key officials in Germany's government and military performed actions that inspired other individuals to perform actions and so forth. In some contexts this sloppiness of language is harmless, but in economic and political debates it can often be harmful. For example, some people think that the "national debt" (by which they mean the debt of the federal government) is harmless because "we owe it to ourselves." In Lesson 22 we expose the flaw in such thinking.

2. Why do statements about a man's actions (implicitly) involve his beliefs as well?

To say that a man acts with a purpose, we are implying that the man believes his action will achieve the result he desires. (If we didn't attribute such a belief to the man, then our description would make no sense.) This seems like a trivial point, but much of the development of economics in the twentieth century involved the growing realization among economists that *expectations* were important. These developments lie outside the scope of this course, but the moral is that these "foundational" issues really do have implications for cutting edge research.

3. Can purposeful action be based on a faulty belief? Give examples.

There are all sorts of examples of purposeful actions that are based on false beliefs. For example, if we see a man on his knee in a fancy restaurant in front of his dinner companion, we might say, "He is proposing to that woman because he wants to spend his life with her." One of his beliefs that motivated this action is that she will say yes. But she very well might say no. Even in that case, the man's action was still purposeful; he just didn't fulfill the purpose as he had expected. In business, entrepreneurs make faulty forecasts all the time. Their actions are still purposeful, and they still fall under the scope of economic theory.

4. What does it mean when economists say preferences are subjective?

This elementary observation simply refers to the fact that people have different tastes. This is a much more straightforward way of explaining market prices, than to assume that these prices are the result of some "objective" facts (such as how much labor went into the product, etc.). The emphasis on subjective preferences will make more sense in Lesson 6 when we explain barter prices.

5. *Does economics say you shouldn't give money to charity?

No! It is perfectly reasonable for an economist to donate money to the poor. The discussion in the text was referring to an *illegitimate application* of economic theory. Specifically, some people learn the "law of diminishing marginal utility" in standard economics courses, and then falsely conclude that a dollar confers less utility on a rich man than on a poor man. This talk is meaningless; economics says no such thing. Now if we want to justify charity on the grounds of moral obligation, that is consistent with economics. The only point here is that standard utility theory does not justify wealth redistribution the way many people think it does.

Supplemental Materials

- Murray Rothbard, *Man, Economy, and State, with Power and Market* (Scholar's Edition, available at **http://mises.org/resources.aspx?Id=e8f5e0fa-d5bb-4844-9a4b-831c6a090d9e**), pp. 1–33.

  > This large volume is Rothbard's grand treatise on economic theory. The serious student who wishes to really master modern Austrian economic thought at some point will have to read Rothbard's book, which is surprisingly easy to read in spite of the complex subject matter. For this course, we are including excerpts to whet the advanced student's appetite and also to give longer discussions on certain points. Another benefit for the advanced student is that Rothbard's terminology and discussion is more formal than the approach taken in this course, and so will provide an easier transition for those students who go on to study economics at a higher level. If the student decides to slog through large portions of Rothbard's treatise, there is also a dedicated study guide available at **http://mises.org/resources/3318/Study-Guide-to-Man-Economy-and-State.**

- Gene Callahan, "Choice and Preference," at **http://mises.org/daily/1163.**

  > In this article, Callahan responds to a famous (within Austrian circles) critique of Austrian economics by Bryan Caplan. The truly advanced student can first read Caplan's critiques (which are linked in the Callahan article), and then read Callahan's response. However, Callahan's article can stand on its own, because he quotes enough from Caplan to get at the heart of the dispute.

Specifically, Caplan had criticized the Austrian approach to choice and preference, which is what we have adopted in this course. Caplan is coming from a mainstream perspective, but Callahan shows that his criticisms misunderstand what the Austrians are saying. This article should be helpful to clarify the relationship between everyday, commonsense concepts and their usage in economic analysis. For example, even though we all know what it means to claim that (say) Mary's preference for vanilla over chocolate is stronger than John's, in economics this statement is meaningless. By the same token, Caplan has focused on the perfectly sensible term of *indifference* from everyday life, but has applied it incorrectly in economics in the Austrian tradition. It's not important for the student to memorize Caplan's specific arguments and Callahan's replies; the important lesson is to understand the framework of choice and preference that Callahan attributes to Mises and his followers.

SUGGESTED ACTIVITIES

Have the student browse a newspaper or watch the nightly news, and note how many times a collective entity (such as a country or government) is reported to have taken a purposeful action.

Subjective or Objective:
Identify the following statements as either subjective or objective.

A. Subjective   B. Objective

1. _____ Pizza is a popular dinner choice amongst Americans.

2. _____ Pepperoni pizza tastes better than just plain cheese pizza.

3. _____ Rap music is disgraceful and delivers a harmful message to children.

4. _____ No singer or band has sold more record units than Elvis Presley.

Matching EssentialTerminology:
Write the appropriate term on the line beside its description.

Quintessence   Preferences   Subjective   Synthesis
Objective   Utility

5. _____ Ranked by people for decision-making.

6. _____ An opinion or matter of taste.

7. _____ A term used to describe how much pleasure or satisfaction a person derives from a particular situation.

8. _____ A fact or precise measurement.

Short Answers (4 points each):
In one to three sentences, respond to the following prompts.

9. Keeping in mind the issue of individuals who act purposefully, rephrase the following statement so that its meaning is more precise.

Germany invaded France in World War II.

_____

_____

_____

10. Guess at Jordan's preference and belief (two separate things) from the following statement.

Jordan took some ibuprofen to ease her pounding head.

_____

_____

_____

11. List your top three books or movies. In making the list, did you have to measure how much enjoyment you got from each book or movie? Explain.

(1) _____

(2) _____

(3) _____

_____

_____

_____

_____

Subjective or Objective:

A. Subjective   B Objective

1. B   2. A

3. A   4. B

Matching Essential Terminology:

5. Preferences

6. Subjective

7. Utility

8. Objective

Short Answers (4 points each):

9. Keeping in mind the issue of individuals who act purposefully, rephrase the following statement so that its meaning is more precise.

Germany invaded France in World War II.

SAMPLE FULL CREDIT ANSWER
During World War II, the leaders of the German government gave orders to military commanders to have their men cross into French territory, fighting any French forces who resisted. Most of the German military men obeyed these orders.

10. Guess at Jordan's preference and belief (two separate things) from the following statement.

Jordan took some ibuprofen to ease her pounding head.

SAMPLE FULL CREDIT ANSWER
Jordan prefers no headache to having a headache, and she believes that taking ibuprofen will eliminate her headache.

11. List your top three books or movies. In making the list, did you have to measure how much enjoyment you got from each book or movie? Explain.

(1) _____

(2) _____

(3) _____

SAMPLE FULL CREDIT ANSWER
I didn't have to measure how much I liked these books/movies. I can rank my preferences even though I can't assign a number to how much I enjoy each one. This is how economists view subjective preferences in general.

SAMPLE PARTIAL CREDIT ANSWER
No I didn't have to.

"Robinson Crusoe" Economics

Introduction

As the student text explains, the purpose of "Robinson Crusoe" economics is to introduce economic concepts in a simplified setting. After the student has mastered the principles in an "economy" consisting of one person, we then generalize it to a real economy with many people.

It used to be common for economics books to use examples of Robinson Crusoe (or perhaps the Swiss Family Robinson) to illustrate ideas, though the practice is rarer now. We have retained the practice for two reasons. First, students seem to respond well to the discussion. Second, the Robinson Crusoe environment is perfect for showing the interaction of natural resources, labor, and capital goods.

Crusoe Creates Goods With His Mind Powers

This section introduces the concept of economic **goods**. The two crucial points are: (1) goods are scarce, and (2) goods are in the eye of the beholder. The first point refers to the fact that there are plenty of conditions or factors in the world, which are definitely useful to humans (gravity, oxygen, etc.). These factors contribute to the satisfaction of people's goals, just as much (or even more so) than things like ladders and apples. But because gravity, oxygen, etc., are (at least in most cases) not scarce, they don't have to be economized, and so don't fall under the umbrella of economic analysis. (Note that some texts might refer to these things as *free goods*, to show that they are still useful but not economic goods.)

The second point ties in with the modern subjective theory of value. Economic goods are defined not by their physical attributes per se, but by the valuing human mind which appraises them.

Consumer Goods versus Producer Goods

This section breaks down the general category of goods into **consumer goods** and **producer goods**. As with the definition of a good in general, here too the distinctions between consumer and producer goods are made in the mind of the beholder; the same physical item can be a consumer good to one person, but a producer good to another.

Land, Labor, and Capital Goods

This section takes producer goods and divides them into finer categories, namely **labor, natural resources** (sometimes called "land"), and **capital goods**. For the truly advanced student, you could mention the technicality that capital goods actually don't need to have been produced by human beings. The *real* criterion of a capital good—as opposed to a natural resource—is its *reproducibility* by humans.

So for example, if Crusoe is planning on cutting down vines, and notices a vine that is perfectly cut just as he would have done himself—perhaps through some animal's gnawing or a fortuitous lightning strike—then he can add that nature-given vine to his stockpile, and consider it another unit of his capital goods. It would be absurd if our definitions required Crusoe to mentally keep track of which vine came from nature, and which he had to transform with his labor and other tools, so that (say) vines #1–14 and #16–27 were capital goods, but vine #15 was a natural resource. If the cut vines are equally useful for the goal Crusoe has in mind—tying sticks together to make a long pole—then economics says they should be units of the same good. The reason the nature-given vine in this case would be a capital good, is that Crusoe can always make more (identical for his purposes) vines if he wants. But we stress that this is a very technical point, and you should only bring it up for an advanced student who won't be confused.

Income, Saving, and Investment

This section is perhaps the single most important one in the entire course, so we encourage you to make sure the student truly understands it. If necessary, you may want to have the student write out the various numerical scenarios, showing how Crusoe allocates his 24 hours for each successive day, how many coconuts he gets to eat each day, and keeping track of his growing stockpile of coconuts. Once Crusoe has accumulated 50 coconuts and begins constructing his pole, the student can also map out what happens each day, to understand what it means to say, "After **saving**, Crusoe **invests** his resources into the construction of a pole."

To underscore the importance of capital maintenance—in other words, the importance of dealing with **depreciation**— you might also have the student map out alternate timelines, showing what happens to Crusoe if he doesn't spend a fifth hour each day working on gathering more vines etc., compared to the timeline sketched out in the text, in which Crusoe establishes a new equilibrium where he maintains the pole in good condition. The student should find that Crusoe can enjoy more leisure in the short run if he ignores depreciation, but then when the pole deteriorates Crusoe faces a crisis and must either sharply cut back on his coconut consumption, or begin drawing down his stockpile. The lesson will obviously apply to a modern economy that goes through a "boom and bust" cycle, as we explain in Lesson 23.

Goods Are Valued Unit by Unit

This section teaches the principle of **marginal utility.** In standard textbooks, they will often teach the related principle of **diminishing marginal utility**, which states that the importance of the last unit of a good drops, as the supply of the good increases. However, we have avoided that terminology, because it can often "teach" the wrong lesson that utility is a quantity of happiness, and that the "number of incremental utils" goes down, as we add more and more units of a good to a stockpile. We are taking pains to avoid this mentality, and that's why we merely describe the principle by saying goods are valued "unit by unit."

The diamond-water paradox is a familiar tool to illustrate the difference between the classical approach to value, versus the modern approach in the wake of the 1870s Marginalist Revolution in economic thought. (If you have not already done so, we recommend again that you watch Joe Salerno's lecture at **http://mises.org/media/4344**.) However, you should be aware that—as with most "revolutions" in any discipline— the classical economists were fully aware of the role that supply and demand played in the different prices for water and diamonds. The problem, though, was that their theoretical framework was ill-suited to handle this complication; they had to overlay the "obvious" facts about relative scarcity on top of their other principles (such as a cost or labor theory of value). The advantage of the modern, subjectivist (and marginalist) approach to explaining economic value is that it more straightforwardly captures the essence of what drives *all* market prices. (If you want to read a journal article dealing with the classical vs. modern approach to pricing theory, try Robert Murphy's exposition here: **http://mises.org/journals/jls/20_1/20_1_3.pdf**. The article eventually gets technical but the beginning will give you a good understanding of how the classical economists explained market prices, and how the modern subjectivist approach is more elegant.)

Pulling It All Together: What Should Crusoe *Do* With Himself?

In this final section, we draw together all the strands of our discussion and argue that Crusoe tries to achieve his more important goals, using the resources at his disposal. (Of course these resources include his labor power.) Be sure that the student understands that costs are fundamentally **opportunity costs**; they are not simply "how much money you have to spend on something." For example, if a woman decides to marry one of several suitors, the true cost of her decision is not simply the money spent on the wedding and reception. No, the true cost *to the woman* of her decision includes the subjective value she places on her next-best alternative, which would either be a different suitor, or deciding not to get married (at that time).

For students who can handle the refinement, you should also stress that costs are *subjective*, not objective facts. To continue with the wedding example, the money spent on the reception is obviously not a "cost" to the bride, if her parents are the ones paying. And even there, it's not the bride's decision that "imposes costs" on the parents, but more accurately it is the parents' decision to follow tradition and kick in the money to pay for their daughter's wedding, once she tells them the news. If her parents were originally planning on using that money for a ski vacation, then the cost *to them of their decision* would be the value each of them placed on going to the vacation. (Note that each parent individually acts and has individual valuations of the ski trip; we are lumping them together for simplicity, to avoid getting into more details about how the family finances are controlled.)

For an advanced student, you could also explain that sometimes the mistake occurs in the opposite direction, where people erroneously conclude that the cost of an action is higher than it really is, because of historical (and irrelevant) money expenditures. For example, if a t-shirt vendor spends $1,000 printing up 500 shirts that say, "Yankees Win!" intending to sell them in the parking lot after the final game of the World Series, he will be devastated if the Yankees in fact lose. Some people would say that he has to charge at least $2 for each shirt, in order to "cover his costs." But that $1,000 is gone, regardless of what he does at this point. (This is typically referred to as a **sunk cost**.) If the vendor finds he can sell the shirts for a dime apiece—perhaps to disappointed fans or to gloating fans of the true victors, who use the shirts in rude ways—that might be his best use of them, in light of the new information. He would probably prefer leaving the parking lot with $50 and no shirts, rather than no money and 500 shirts that he can use as rags at home. So the true cost of his decision to sell the shirts for a dime apiece is *not* $950 (= $1,000 - $50), but rather the subjective value the man would have received from having an additional 500 rags at home. That's why it is still beneficial for him to sell the shirts "at a loss," because the decision *at that point* confers higher benefits than costs. (These issues are explored in the reading on marginality in the Supplemental Materials.)

•
STUDY QUESTIONS

1. Does economics assume that people act in isolation from the rest of society?

No, the point of studying Robinson Crusoe is simply to keep the analysis as simple as possible for the student. In the next part of the book, we will explain the operation of a market economy, which is composed of many people. However, the same principles that apply to Crusoe also apply to individuals in a market—the presence of other people is simply another feature of the environment, as it were.

2. What does it mean to say Crusoe creates goods with his "mind powers"?

Obviously we do not mean that Crusoe has magical powers to conjure up coconuts through thought. What we meant by this section title is that coconuts (or vines, sticks, etc.) are not goods merely because of their intrinsic properties. In order to become economic goods, someone (Crusoe in this case) has to use his mind to *classify* them as scarce objects that can help him achieve his objectives.

3. Can leisure be more physically demanding than work?

Yes, as a footnote explained, it's possible that Crusoe enjoys swimming in the ocean as a leisure activity. This is much more physically taxing than other chores such as gathering twigs for a fire. Presumably Crusoe does not derive *direct* pleasure from collecting twigs, and so this activity is *work*, not leisure.

4. Why does Crusoe need to worry about depreciation of his capital goods?

If Crusoe ignores the wearing away of the pole, he will experience a sudden drop in his consumption. After going to the trouble of investing in capital goods, Crusoe needs to maintain them (by investing enough to offset depreciation) if he wants to remain at his higher standard of living.

5. How do expectations affect someone's decisions?

The term *expectations* is simply economist jargon for forecasts. For every action, a person relies on his or her forecasts of the future; that's the whole point of acting, to try to influence future events. The text dealt with an example of Crusoe building a raft, only to realize he couldn't get out to the open sea. But even more mundane actions rely on expectations. For example, Crusoe "expects" that if he climbs a tree, he will be able to knock coconuts down, and that the coconuts will not be full of spiders when he cracks them open.

Supplemental Materials

- Gene Callahan, *Economics for Real People*, Chapter 3.

  Callahan adapts the television reality show "Survivor" for his own version of Robinson Crusoe economics.

- Robert Murphy, "What Does Marginality Mean?" at **http:// mises.org/daily/1584.**

  Murphy lays out some of the implications of "thinking on the margin." There is discussion here of "sunk cost" fallacies, which interest some students but are not essential for the course.

- Murray Rothbard, *Man, Economy, and State*, pp. 42–72.

  The material does not coincide perfectly with the layout in this course, but the student who finds Rothbard useful will eventually hit most of the same points if he or she follows along with the pages as listed in the Supplemental Materials outline.

- Murray Rothbard, "Introduction to Economics: Part I," audio at **http://mises.org/media/4454**.

  Rothbard's lecturing style leads him on many interesting tangents that the beginning student need not pursue, but even so this introductory lecture discusses Crusoe economics and may be easier for some students to digest than Rothbard's formal treatise.

SUGGESTED ACTIVITIES

(1) Ask the student to think of situations in which typically non-scarce goods can become scarce and hence subject to economic analysis. For example, deep sea divers must purchase tanks of oxygen, and we could imagine space travelers buying gravity-generating devices for their ships.

(2) Ask the student to come up with scenarios in which changing beliefs can alter which physical things are considered scarce economic goods. For example, if a certain root is believed to have medicinal properties, people will pay others to collect it. But if it turns out that the man publicizing the claims is a fraud, then the root might lose its status as a good.

(3) The next time you and the student are at a store, ask about the status of the items on the shelf, from the point of view of the store owner and the customer. For example, the student could say that all of the items on the shelves are producer goods to the owner, because he or she looks at them as a means of earning money. But from the point of view of the customer, some of the items (such as a loaf of bread) could be classified as a consumer good, while others (such as a drill) could be classified either way, depending on how the student frames the situation. (Note that in one sense, a drill doesn't confer *direct* happiness on the consumer, except in a Tim Allen-macho-man fashion.) Furthermore, even "obvious" consumer goods could be classified as producer goods, depending on how the student frames the issue. A woman might buy expensive clothes in order to fit in with a certain group of people, for example, even though she would rather wear sweatpants; in this sense the items are a means to an end, i.e., producer goods.

(4) Have the student draw up a 7-day plan for Crusoe in the new equilibrium, showing exactly how he allocates his hours each day in a typical week, so that the supply of coconuts never drops below 100. (A footnote in the text sketches the answer.)

Producer or Consumer Good:
Identify the following as (most likely) producer or consumer goods.

A. Producer good(s)   B. Consumer good(s)

1. _____ A glass of iced tea.

2. _____ Robinson Crusoe's coconuts.

3. _____ Robinson Crusoe's long stick.

4. _____ A paring knife.

Matching Essential Terminology:
Write the appropriate term on the line beside its description.

Economize	Goods	Land/Natural Resources
Labor	Income	Opportunity Cost
Saving	Investment	Equilibrium
Marginal Utility	Capital Goods	Equivocate

5. _____ The subjective value placed on the next-best alternative that must be sacrificed in any choice.

6. _____ The flow of productive services performed with your body.

7. _____ The evaluation of the importance of goods on a unit by unit basis.

8. _____ To use resources being mindful of their scarcity.

9. _____ Factors of production that are created by people.

10. _____ Scarce items that can help a person achieve his or her goals.

11. _____ When someone consumes less than his or her income.

12. _____ When factors of production are devoted to future income, rather than immediate consumption.

Short Answers (4 points each):
In one to three sentences, respond to the following prompts.

13. Explain why an object only becomes a good when a person incorporates it into his plans.

_____

_____

_____

_____

_____

_____

_____

14. Identify the distinction between a producer and a consumer good.

_____

_____

_____

_____

_____

_____

_____

15. Explain why a person in Robinson Crusoe's position would want, on any given day, to harvest more coconuts than he or she planned on consuming that day.

_____

_____

_____

_____

_____

_____

_____

_____

_____

_____

16. Water is necessary for life, but restaurants give it away for free. Diamonds are mere décor, serving only vanity, but they cannot be had cheaply. Explain this so-called "water–diamond paradox."

_____

_____

_____

_____

_____

_____

_____

_____

_____

_____

17. Explain the following scenario.

Rory looked at the mess that the burglars had made, sat down on the edge of his bed and wept. The thieves had made away with three hundred dollars in cash, his laptop, his iPod, his Xbox 360, and all of his games; but that's not why he wept. More than any of those expensive items, Rory most regretted the theft of his father's class ring. It was only ten carat gold, and the red center stone wasn't even a real ruby. No pawnshop would have given him more than fifty dollars for the ring, but it was the loss of this ring that now left Rory emotionally distraught.

_____

_____

_____

_____

_____

_____

_____

_____

_____

_____

_____

_____

_____

_____

Producer or Consumer Good:

A. Producer good(s)   B. Consumer good(s)

1. B   2. B   3. A   4. A

Matching Essential Terminology:

5. Opportunity Cost   6. Labor

7. Marginal Utility   8. Economize

9. Capital goods   10. Goods

11. Saving   12. Investment

Short Answers (4 points each):

13. Explain why an object only becomes a good when a person incorporates it into his plans.

SAMPLE FULL CREDIT ANSWER
Something is a good not because of its physical properties, but because a person subjectively values it. If people didn't enjoy smoking, then tobacco would cease being a (production) good and would be the equivalent of a weed. A person values an object as a good because the person has a plan in which that object will help to achieve a goal.

SAMPLE PARTIAL CREDIT ANSWER
A person gives value to a good by thinking about it.

SAMPLE NO CREDIT ANSWER
If a person has to come up with a plan to obtain an object—such as Crusoe having to assemble sticks and vines to knock down coconuts—then the object becomes a good.

14. Identify the distinction between a producer and a consumer good.

SAMPLE FULL CREDIT ANSWER
A consumer good directly satisfies goals or preferences. A producer good isn't directly useful, but it can be used to make other producer goods or consumer goods.

SAMPLE NO CREDIT ANSWER
A producer good is made by businesses.

15. Explain why a person in Robinson Crusoe's position would want, on any given day, to harvest more coconuts than he or she planned on consuming that day.

SAMPLE FULL CREDIT ANSWER
By producing more than he consumes, Crusoe can save coconuts over time. This stockpile of savings will help Crusoe if he gets sick or wants to take a day off in the future. It will also allow Crusoe to spend his work days making tools instead of collecting coconuts with his bare hands.

SAMPLE PARTIAL CREDIT ANSWER
This way Crusoe can save.

SAMPLE NO CREDIT ANSWER
Crusoe might have made a mistake in how hungry he thought he would be.

16. Water is necessary for life, but restaurants give it away for free. Diamonds are mere décor, serving only vanity, but they cannot be had cheaply. Explain this so-called "water–diamond paradox."

SAMPLE FULL CREDIT ANSWER
People evaluate goods on the margin. No one chooses between all the water in the world and all the diamonds. Diamonds are much scarcer than water, because their total supply can't satisfy all the desires for it, but water is relatively much more plentiful.

SAMPLE PARTIAL CREDIT ANSWER
There is more water than diamonds.

SAMPLE NO CREDIT ANSWER
Restaurants wouldn't sell any water if they charged too much for it.

17. Explain the following scenario.

Rory looked at the mess that the burglars had made . . .

SAMPLE FULL CREDIT ANSWER
People don't care simply about the market value of things, they also value items for emotional reasons. Rory could eventually replace the other items over time by buying new ones. But he won't be able to replace the lost ring, even though he would be willing to pay a lot of money to do so.

Part II

CAPITALISM:
THE MARKET ECONOMY

The Institution of Private Property

Society Requires Rules

To reinforce the connection between Lesson 4 and Part II, you may want to stress this opening section. The general principles we discussed regarding Crusoe still apply to him, once he returns to civilization. In other words, it's not that the rules of Lesson 4 only work on tropical islands with one inhabitant.

However, there is a problem once we recognize that in a modern city, there are millions of Crusoes walking around, appraising goods and trying to achieve their most preferred goals. To settle conflicts, people assign **property rights** to scarce goods. It's not so much that the laws of economics need to be altered to deal with a modern market economy. It's more accurate to say that the existence of property rights (with their corresponding "rules of engagement") provide a new form of tradeoffs or constraints that each "Crusoe" must take into account when making decisions.

To help the student see the big picture, make sure he or she understands the layout of the text. Part I laid out the nature and scope of economic theory, and then applied it (in Lesson 4) to the case of an isolated individual. Part II sketches the operation of a pure market economy, in which everything is privately owned (and we simply assume people respect property rights). Part III briefly describes the operation of pure socialism, in which the government effectively controls all natural resources and capital goods. Finally, in Part IV we describe a mixed economy, in which the government heavily intervenes to influence the outcome of the underlying capitalist economy.

In an introductory course, we will rely on specific numerical examples and hypothetical illustrations of particular concepts. We are not trying to formally "prove" the validity of particular laws or principles. Even so, it's important that the student does not get the impression that economic science "only works in a capitalist system." No, the underlying economic principles apply to all people and all societies. But the institutional setting can certainly influence the *results* of these fundamental concepts, as we will see. For an analogy, it would be silly to say that the principles of biology only apply to a planet that receives as much sunshine as Earth does; obviously biology doesn't "assume" a particular amount of sunlight. Even so, biology certainly *can* inform us that if all sunlight were suddenly blocked, then most life on Earth would quickly die.

Capitalism: This Is Private Property

Part II of the book sketches the operation of a pure capitalist system, in which *everything* is owned by private individuals. Note that there can still be group ownership under capitalism. For example, business partners can jointly own the assets of their company, and numerous shareholders can collectively own a single corporation.

If there is any risk of confusion, you may need to clarify that just because someone is the legal owner of a good, doesn't absolve him or her of all moral and religious obligations. For example, even if someone owns his own body, and has the legal right to shave his head or to get a vulgar tattoo, it may still violate his religious beliefs to do so. It wouldn't be a valid argument against his religious peers to say, "I'm the owner so you can't tell me what to do with my hair!"

In an introductory course, we are not dealing with exotic applications of private property, such as private ownership of roads, or even private ownership of tanks and aircraft carriers. This is not a course on political philosophy so we are not addressing the important questions of the proper role of government in society. Rather, we are sketching the operation of a pure market economy in order to show the student "raw" capitalism in contrast to other institutional settings, and to understand some of the economic effects of handling particular resources through private property, government ownership, or a mixture of the two.

The Market Economy and Free Enterprise

It is important that the student realize "the market" does not refer to a place, even though he or she might have gone to a "farmers' market" at some point. In our context, "the market" is shorthand for the market economy, which includes all of the exchanges in a region. In modern times, most of the entire world falls into one giant market (subject to heavy interference from governments). Even though we often speak of the U.S. economy, the Japanese economy, and so forth, strictly speaking international trade connects almost all consumers and producers around the world into one nexus. If, say, Japanese factories begin using more oil, that will lead to higher gasoline prices for American motorists than would otherwise be the case.

You should stress the significance of free enterprise, for it is a remarkable achievement that is taken for granted. At first blush, it's simply extraordinary that a capitalist system can allow people the freedom to pick whatever jobs they want. After all, what if not enough people become farmers, or engineers, or doctors...? In later lessons we will explain how market prices (especially wage rates and salaries) steer people into occupations where they are needed, but for now you should at least point out to the student that the very idea of free enterprise is extraordinary.

• •

STUDY QUESTIONS

1. Did Crusoe need an institution of private property?

No, the only conflict Crusoe had was with Nature. If he wanted more coconuts to eat, he simply had to decide whether the benefits outweighed the additional sacrifice of leisure. There were no other intelligences who may have had their own designs on the scarce goods.

2. Why does economic scarcity lead to potential conflict in society?

Scarcity means that there aren't enough units of a good (or service) to satisfy everyone's potential uses for it. In society, people often have incompatible aims for the same unit of a good. (If Jim eats a piece of pizza, Sally can't eat the same piece.)

3. What are the three main institutional settings we will study in this course?

Pure capitalism, pure socialism, and the mixed economy (as defined in the student text and also above).

4. Is the sketch of a pure market economy a realistic depiction of the United States?

Not at all! Historically, the United States was the closest to a large, pure capitalist economy the world has ever known, but the U.S. federal government has grown steadily since its birth. Even though many people consider the United States in the early 21st century to be an illustration of the operation of capitalism, in our terminology it is most definitely a mixed economy.

5. What does it mean when an economist says, "We should let the market decide"?

Such a statement means that the government should not inter-fere with the outcome of voluntary interactions among private property owners. It's important for students to realize that letting "the market" decide something isn't ceding decision-making authority away from concerned individuals and into the hands of a lifeless concept. On the contrary, "the market" in this context refers to the decisions made by certain individ-uals in the private sector, and any government involvement would simply substitute the desires of government officials for the people in the private sector. Decisions are always made by individuals.

Supplemental Materials

- Ludwig von Mises, *Human Action* (Scholar's Edition, available at **http://mises.org/resources/3250**), Chapter XV, Section 1, pp. 258–60, 264–70.

  As should be clear by now, this course relies heavily on the work of economist Ludwig von Mises. Unfortunately, Mises's writing can be quite difficult for a newcomer, because not only is his language very formal, but he also assumes that his readers are familiar with a wide range of subjects. Even so, advanced students should at least try to read the excerpts from Mises's *magnum opus, Human Action.* Assure them that even professional Austrian economists can struggle with some portions of the book, but it is worth sampling because of its importance in the development of the modern Austrian School. For students who want to jump in, there is a study guide to the book at **http://mises.org/ books/humanactionstudy.pdf**.

- Thomas DiLorenzo, "Capitalism, Our Benefactor," audio at **http://mises.org/media/1367.**

  This is an easy-to-follow talk by an economist who writes extensively on American history. Students should enjoy the familiar historical episodes presented (perhaps) in a radically new light.

- Ralph Raico, "Liberalism," video at **http://mises.org/ media/4358.**

  Historian Ralph Raico lays out the principles of classical liberalism, referring to the program of capitalism, reason, limited government, and peace among nations, that Mises and others tried to defend in the twentieth century against the competing ideas of socialism and (what would now be called) progressivism. Note that the modern term "liberalism"—to describe for example the political views of the late Sen. Ted Kennedy—is not at all the same as the classical liberalism that Raico describes.

SUGGESTED ACTIVITIES

(1) Especially if the student is an animal lover, you could ask whether it's really correct to say that Crusoe was the only intelligent mind on his island, appraising the scarce goods. For example, what if Crusoe's activities destroyed bird nests? There is no preferred answer here, but you should point out the difficulties in actually assigning property rights to birds, monkeys, etc. Note too that just because someone has the legal right to use an object (i.e., is its owner), doesn't relieve him or her of moral or religious responsibilities. For example, even if we can agree that Crusoe is the effective owner of everything on the island, we can still consider it deeply immoral for him to commit wanton cruelty to the animals on it.

(2) One of the most difficult problems in applying the concept of private property in the real world, is understanding the boundaries between various property rights. A discussion on these issues might be fruitful. The classic expression of this idea is to say, "Your right to extend your fist ends where my nose begins," but there are many other examples. For example, does a homeowner have the right to throw a noisy party on his own property at 3 a.m., or do his neighbors have the right to exclude disturbing sound vibrations from entering *their* property? These subtleties lie outside the scope of this course, but they could provoke interesting discussions. Murray Rothbard laid out a particular view of property rights in his book *The Ethics of Liberty*, at **http://mises. org/rothbard/ethics/ethics.asp**. Note that not all libertarian or even Austrian scholars would necessarily endorse Rothbard's views, but the book at least provides an example of a serious attempt to answer the question of assigning actual property titles.

TEST — LESSON 5
THE INSTITUTION OF PRIVATE PROPERTY

Multiple Choice: Choose the best answer.

1. The capitalist system is based upon
    A. trade protection.
    B. trade surpluses.
    C. private property.
    D. government intervention.

2. Capitalism was originally a smear used by which socialist founder?
    A. Adam Smith
    B. Jean-Jacques Rousseau
    C. Vladimir Lenin
    D. Karl Marx
    E. Paul Krugman

3. These were medieval associations of craftsmen designed to limit competition in a certain trades.
    A. guilds
    B. temperance societies
    C. inquisitions
    D. labor unions

4. The system in which individuals may choose to enter any line of work that they so choose is called
    A. Crusoe economics.
    B. mixed market.
    C. free enterprise.
    D. socialism.

Matching Essential Terminology:
Write the appropriate term on the line beside its description.

Market

Free Enterprise

Guilds

Slavery

Private Property

5. _____ An association of craftsmen that regulates competition.

6. _____ The institution assigning ownership of goods to specific individuals.

7. _____ The whole web of exchanges that individuals make with their private property.

8. _____ When some individuals have the legal right to the bodies and services of other individuals.

9. Explain why the boundaries imposed by property ownership are absolutely essential to a capitalist system.

_____

_____

_____

_____

_____

_____

_____

_____

_____

10. Explain how property rights minimize conflicts.

_____

_____

_____

_____

_____

_____

_____

_____

Multiple Choice:

1. C   2. D   3. A   4. C

Matching Essential Terminology: Write the best term on the line beside its description.

5. Guilds

6. Private Property

7. Market

8. Slavery

9. Explain why the boundaries imposed by property ownership are absolutely essential to a capitalist system.

SAMPLE FULL CREDIT ANSWER
Capitalism gives people the freedom to start any business or to work for any employer that they desire. Consumers are also free to buy or not buy whatever products and services they desire. The only way this system can work is if there are strict boundaries on who owns what, so that it is clear which person has the right to use or trade away a particular good.

SAMPLE PARTIAL CREDIT ANSWER
If people didn't get to keep the fruits of their labor, they would have no reason to work hard.

SAMPLE NO CREDIT ANSWER
If there weren't private property, it would be socialism or communism.

10. Explain how property rights minimize conflicts.

SAMPLE FULL CREDIT ANSWER
Resources are scarce, meaning that there aren't enough to satisfy everyone's desires for using those resources. This situation leads to conflict, because if one person uses a good to satisfy his goals, someone else won't be able to. Property rights provide an orderly way to determine which person gets to decide how a good will be used, and how that ownership can be transferred to a different person.

SAMPLE PARTIAL CREDIT ANSWER
Without property rights, people would always fight over resources.

SAMPLE NO CREDIT ANSWER
People won't be jealous about other people's wealth if they have property of their own.

Direct Exchange and Barter Prices

Why Do People Trade With Each Other?

One of the most crucial principles in all of modern economics is that both parties benefit from a voluntary exchange. (Or more precisely, both parties *expect* to benefit.) For the purists, note that technically we mean benefit *on net*, or in other words, both parties expect the benefits to outweigh the costs when they engage in a voluntary trade.

This is possible because preferences are subjective. For example, it would not be possible for both parties in a trade to walk away with a heavier object than each started out with. That's because weight is an objective fact, an intrinsic property of an object. In contrast, value is in the mind of the beholder, and that's why two people can both feel they gave up something of lesser value, in exchange for something of greater value, when they make a voluntary trade.

The text mentions the caveat that the parties *expect* to benefit. This is because, after the fact, one or both parties might regret the decision. For example, if someone sells a parcel of land for a certain sum of money, and then later discovers that there was a large oil deposit on the property, the seller will probably regret the earlier decision.

Direct Exchange / Barter

Even though many textbooks jump right into a discussion of exchanges against units of money, in this course we opt to start with barter. There are several reasons for this. First, trading with money is simply a special case of the principles we develop in this chapter; in other words, everything we say in the analysis of barter prices is true for money, because units of money are units of a (very special) good. Second, historically people must have traded with each other in barter, before they began using money. Third, we want to show that money emerged spontaneously through market exchanges—not from the edicts of a government official—in Lesson 7. But in order for that demonstration to make sense, the student will first need to understand the formation of barter prices which we develop in the current chapter.

Be sure that the student isn't confused by the term *direct exchange*, since we earlier defined a consumption good as one that confers *direct* utility or satisfaction. As we point out in the text, even though a producer good only confers indirect utility or satisfaction (e.g., you can't eat a tractor, but you can use it to harvest more food), even so a producer good can still be acquired through direct exchange. So the contrast between *direct* and *indirect* means different things, in the context of consumer versus producer goods, and direct versus indirect exchanges.

Prices

The material in this section is fairly straightforward. Just make sure the student understands that money is a good, and why we can reverse prices as we normally express them to talk about how many units of some other good (cars, bubble gum, etc.) one needs to sell in order to "buy" one unit of money. For example, if a car's price is $15,000, then that is equivalent to saying that a car dealer needs to sell 1/15,000th of a car to buy one dollar. If that seems too contrived because no one sells fractional cars, you can use an example of a good that costs less than $1. For example, if we are dealing with a pack of chewing gum that sells for 50 cents, then the seller of the gum must sell two packs in order to buy one dollar bill.

As we will make clearer in Lesson 7, one of the great virtues of trading with money is that people only need to keep track of one price for every good. In an economy with 20 goods (not counting the money good), using money means that people only need to stay up to speed with 20 different price ratios. In barter, in principle they would need to stay aware of 190 independent ratios. This is because there are 20x19=380 total arrangements of goods, taken two at a time. However, half of those prices would be redundant, because if a trader knows the banana:orange price ratio, he can simply use division to obtain the orange:banana ratio.

How Prices Are Formed in Barter

As the text says in a footnote, the material in this section might be too difficult for some students. However, we suggest that you urge even hesitant students to at least work through the section, even if they don't fully absorb all the details. Once the student understands how the tables work (which may require help from you), the narrative should be fairly intuitive.

Notice that the explanation of barter price formation in this section relies very heavily on the fact that preferences are *rankings*, not measurements. Nowhere in this section do we use "utility functions" or assign a total "enjoyment number" to a particular combination of candy bars. All we need to assume is that the siblings can rank various combinations of candy bars in order of most to least preferred, and that is sufficient to discuss equilibrium barter prices.

Be sure the student understands the reason for making Alice and Billy's preferences identical. We are showing that different initial endowments of candy can yield gains from trade. In other words, it wouldn't be so surprising if a Snickers-lover could make mutually advantageous deals with a Milky Way-lover. But the student might not have realized that because goods are valued on the margin (or unit by unit), even people with identical preference rankings can still gain from trade (if they start with different combinations of goods).

To avoid confusion, you might want to tell the student that there are no "rules" on preferences in the real world. In our numerical examples, Alice, Billy, and Christy exhibit obvious patterns in their preference rankings for candy bars. We did this so as not to overwhelm the student, and also to crisply illustrate the influence of different tendencies (such as desire for more candy and for variety). In the real world, people don't have to justify or explain their preferences according to particular forces that "generate" them.

The student text should be self-explanatory, once one knows how to read the tables. If necessary, you may need to copy the relevant pages (or print them from the online version) in order for the student to be able to refer easily back and forth between the text's discussion and the relevant table. Although the process may seem tedious to some students at first, the ultimate payoff should make it worthwhile. Many readers will probably be surprised at the end of the chapter when they realize they completely understand every aspect of the "market" where Snickers are sold against Milky Ways (and vice versa). The discussion quickly changes from some truisms about children and candy bars, into general insights about markets.

For the advanced student, you should be clear as to exactly what we have shown in this section. We did not prove that the children had to exchange their candy bars according to one of the described equilibrium scenarios. As the text explains, even if the children really had the preferences we ascribed to them, it would still be possible for them to fail to trade at all, because of strategic miscalculations. It's also possible that two children could make a trade that the third party would have liked to stop with a counteroffer, but failed to act in time. In that sense, two of the children could regret a voluntary trade that one of them made with the third child, even though the child making the trade thought it was a good idea at the time.

Some textbooks might describe the equilibrium outcomes as ones that would be likely to occur if the children showed up day after day with the same preferences and the same initial holdings of candy. However, even that isn't quite right, because then children might be tempted to engage in long-range strategic ploys, playing hardball in the first few rounds in order to obtain better trading terms later on. We think it's simplest just to say that the equilibrium outcomes we've sketched are the ones in which there are no further gains from trade, and in which no one regrets the trades in light of new information (such as a third child saying, "Why did you sell for such a low price?!").

Collapsing the Scope of Prices By Adding More Traders

The material in this final subsection is the hardest of the chapter. If a student is lost, you can safely omit the discussion concerning "knocking out" equilibrium prices with the arrival of Christy. However, even for such a student you should at least have him study the discussion of the equilibrium (with all three children) where 1 Snickers trades for 2 Milky Ways, in which Alice sells 2 Snickers and buys 4 Milky Ways, while Billy and Christy each buy 1 Snickers and sell 2 Milky Ways. This discussion ties all the strands together and shows a complete market from a bird's eye perspective.

● ●

STUDY QUESTIONS

1. How is it possible for both parties to benefit from the same exchange?

Economic value is subjective.

2. *If a producer good only provides benefits indirectly, can a producer good be obtained via direct exchange?

Yes. The text discusses the example of a farmer trading away bacon for tomato seeds, which are presumably a producer good (intended for planting to yield tomatoes). So long as both farmers intend on using the obtained goods themselves (rather than trading them away yet again), the exchange is a direct one. (The distinction between direct and indirect exchange will be much clearer after you work through Lesson 7.)

3. Suppose the economy has only four goods: apples, oranges, bananas, and grapes. In barter, how many independent price ratios would exist? (E.g., the apple:orange ratio would not be independent of the orange:apple ratio.)

There are 4x3=12 different pairs of goods, but only 6 if the order is unimportant. So in a barter economy with four goods, traders would need to keep track of 6 different price ratios. Specifically, they are: apples:oranges, apples:bananas, apples:grapes, oranges:bananas, oranges:grapes, and bananas:grapes. (If you know that 1 apple trades for 2 bananas, then you automatically know that 1 banana trades for half an apple. That's why you only need to keep track of 6 total exchange ratios in this small economy.)

4. If Alice likes Snickers more than Milky Ways, does that mean she would always choose a Snickers over a Milky Way, if offered a choice between one or the other?

No, because she might start out with more Snickers than Milky Ways. For example, if Alice starts out with (2 Snickers and 0 Milky Ways), she would rather obtain one additional Milky Way than one additional Snickers. The former gift would raise her to the 14th spot on her preference ranking, whereas the latter would raise her only to the 19th. (She would start at the 21st spot.) Note that in a sense, it's inaccurate to say "Alice likes Snickers more than Milky Ways" for this very reason, but of course in everyday language we speak like this all the time.

5. *In what sense did Christy's arrival "knock out" some of the possible equilibrium prices that could have formed between Alice and Billy?

All we mean is that Christy would be willing to make counteroffers to prevent some of the original equilibrium trading outcomes from occurring. Intuitively, Alice wouldn't sell Snickers at such low prices to Billy once Christy enters the scene with her stockpile of Milky Ways and her tendency to prefer Snickers.

Supplemental Materials

- Gene Callahan, *Economics for Real People*, Chapter 4.

    Callahan outlines the basics of direct exchange. Reading his chapter 4 in conjunction with this course's Lesson 6 may help the students to really grasp the material. However, Callahan begins his chapter with a discussion of the division of labor, a topic we won't cover until Lesson 8.

- Murray Rothbard, *Man, Economy, and State*, pp. 84–94, 103–26.

    For advanced students who want a more thorough treatment, the Rothbard excerpts provide a more standard exposition based on the historical development of the theory of barter pricing in economic thought. However, you should be warned that Rothbard's tables do not work the same way as the ones in this course. Rather than listing all possible combinations of goods, Rothbard instead constructs preference rankings (or "value scales") based on the person's original holdings. Then he uses parentheses to indicate items that are not yet in the person's possession. The underlying principles are the same, but some students may be confused by the different technique for depicting preferences. The advantage of the method we have adopted in this book is that it quite clearly shows the ranking of various hypothetical outcomes, but the advantage of Rothbard's approach is that he can handle larger quantities of goods and thus give more realistic numerical examples.

SUGGESTED ACTIVITIES

(1) If you have more than one student, an obvious activity would be to create your own market using candy bars (or some other goods that you deem more appropriate). You could try to demonstrate the effect of different initial endowments by conducting the trials over several days. On Day 1, you might give some students nothing but Snickers, while others are given nothing but Milky Ways. Record who was given what, and then record the outcome of their voluntary transactions. On Day 2, you could reverse the initial distribution, and see what difference it may have made. (Ideally you would use the bite-size bars, and not give so many that the students would carry them forward to the next day and possibly disrupt the "experiment.") Of course this wouldn't be a truly controlled experiment, because the students' preferences could change from day to day, and their bargaining strategies could also evolve as they gain experience. Even so, it might be interesting to document actual barter price formation with goods that they really value. Implementing the candy bar market for real would also drive home the point that (with three or more students) you need to set up procedures for how trades will be conducted. To keep things as close to the text discussion as possible, you might be an umpire and allow any student to offer a trade to another, but then give all other students a chance to make a counteroffer if they think allowing the announced trade to go through would hurt their position.

(2) If you have at least four students, you could also try conducting different trials in which the students are isolated in smaller markets on Day 1, and then all lumped together in a single market on Day 2. It would be very interesting to see if the same Snickers:Milky Way price were established in each of the smaller markets on Day 1, and (if not) what price was established in Day 2 in the big market including all students.

Short Answer:
On the lines provided, answer the questions in 1 to 3 sentences.

1. Explain how, at the moment of exchange, both parties in a voluntary trade expect to benefit from it.

_____

_____

_____

_____

_____

_____

_____

_____

2. Suppose a farmer trades the metalsmith 10 pigs to obtain an axe that the farmer will use to chop down trees. The metalsmith intends to keep the pigs and eventually eat them. Is this a direct or indirect exchange? Explain your answer.

_____

_____

_____

_____

_____

_____

_____

_____

3. How does subjective value make "gains from trade" possible?

_____

_____

_____

_____

_____

_____

_____

_____

4. In the Halloween candy example, what did we mean by an "equilibrium position" or "equilibrium price"? Was the textbook saying that such an outcome had to occur?

_____

_____

_____

_____

_____

_____

_____

_____

_____

_____

5. Do people need money in order for market prices to form? Explain.

_____

_____

_____

_____

_____

_____

_____

_____

_____

_____

_____

Short Answer:

1. Explain how, at the moment of exchange, both parties in a voluntary trade expect to benefit from it.

SAMPLE FULL CREDIT ANSWER
If a trade is voluntary, it means that both parties agree to it, that neither is being forced into making the trade. Therefore, it must be the case that each party expects to benefit from it in some sense.

SAMPLE PARTIAL CREDIT ANSWER
People are usually pretty good at knowing what they like.

SAMPLE NO CREDIT ANSWER
If people make a trade, we know they must benefit from it.

2. Suppose a farmer trades the metalsmith 10 pigs to obtain an axe that the farmer will use to chop down trees. The metalsmith intends to keep the pigs and eventually eat them. Is this a direct or indirect exchange? Explain your answer.

SAMPLE FULL CREDIT ANSWER
A direct exchange occurs when both parties intend to personally use the item received, either for consumption or production. Since the farmer wants to use the axe to cut down trees, and the metal-smith wants to eat the pigs, this qualifies as a direct exchange.

SAMPLE PARTIAL CREDIT ANSWER
This is a direct exchange because the metalsmith eats the pigs, rather than selling the bacon to others.

SAMPLE NO CREDIT ANSWER
This is an indirect exchange, because the farmer doesn't directly benefit from having an axe, he instead benefits from having more firewood. The axe is a tool to reach his ultimate goal, so this is an indirect exchange.

3. How does subjective value make "gains from trade" possible?

SAMPLE FULL CREDIT ANSWER
"Gains from trade" mean that both parties are better off after making a trade. This is possible because the value each person places on the goods being traded is subjective. For example, Jim can value Mary's bologna sandwich more than his peanut butter sandwich, while Mary can have the opposite preference, meaning that both can walk away from the trade with a good possessing higher value.

SAMPLE PARTIAL CREDIT ANSWER
People will only make a trade if they expect to benefit from it.

SAMPLE NO CREDIT ANSWER
When people make trades, it shows the items have equal value. For example, if someone spends $15 on a DVD, then the DVD has a value of $15.

4. In the Halloween candy example, what did we mean by an "equilibrium position" or "equilibrium price"? Was the textbook saying that such an outcome had to occur?

SAMPLE FULL CREDIT ANSWER
An equilibrium occurred when there were no more gains from trade available, and where nobody could make a better offer to prevent the actual trades from occurring. This outcome was "stable" because if the kids began going down this path, there would be no reason for the kids to stray from it. The textbook was not saying that real-world children would necessarily trade their candy according to such an equilibrium, because (for example) the kids might make mistakes in their negotiation strategies, and end up having someone "call their bluff."

SAMPLE PARTIAL CREDIT ANSWER
An equilibrium occurred after all the trades were made.

SAMPLE NO CREDIT ANSWER
The textbook defined an equilibrium as an ideal or optimal distribution of the candy among the children.

5. Do people need money in order for market prices to form? Explain.

SAMPLE FULL CREDIT ANSWER

No, market prices are simply exchange ratios in trades between different goods. Money is very useful to facilitate trades, but it is not necessary. The Halloween candy example doesn't use money, but it shows how prices form.

SAMPLE PARTIAL CREDIT ANSWER

No, there is barter.

SAMPLE NO CREDIT ANSWER

Yes, in a modern economy prices are quoted in money.

Indirect Exchange and the Appearance of Money

or this chapter you should understand some technical distinctions to place this material in context with other books. Most economists use the term *barter* to refer to any *non-monetary* exchange. Therefore, a "barter economy" under this broad definition would still allow for people to use media of exchange, that is, to engage in indirect exchanges.

For advanced students, you should therefore be careful in the presentation of the material below, especially the first section. There, we are showing the limitations of a world strictly confined to *direct* exchange. Notice that this is more restrictive than a world confined merely to barter. In other words, in our considerations of "The Limitations of Direct Exchange," we aren't just ruling out the use of money, we are going much further and ruling out the use of any medium of exchange at all. This is a harsher condition, because money is a very special *kind* of medium of exchange, namely one that is accepted by almost everyone in the community.

Then, in the middle of the lesson, we introduce generic indirect exchange, but do not yet suppose that there is *one* medium of exchange involved in every transaction. This is a subtle point, but should help advanced students clarify their thinking. (It is also related to the 5th study question.)

Finally, at the end of the lesson we explore an economy that not only has indirect exchange (i.e., where people use media of exchange, that is, where they accept some things in trade with the intention of trading them away to a third party), but goes further and uses money. To repeat, a monetary economy is a very special case of an economy that practices indirect exchange. So there are not three categories here, only two: Direct and indirect exchange. Monetary exchange falls into the latter category, but we can imagine indirect exchanges that do not involve money.

The Limitations of Direct Exchange

It is common to explain the limitations of direct exchange by citing its need for a "double coincidence of wants." For example, in order for a dentist to get bread, he has to find a baker with a toothache. Most textbooks (if they even mention this) drop the matter there, and assume the case for money has been made.

However, the Austrian School economists tend to push the analysis much deeper, showing that business production itself would be impractical in a world of direct exchange. This is partly due to the fact that Carl Menger, the founder of the Austrian School, discovered the mechanism by which money could spontaneously develop in a market originally limited to direct exchange, and so Austrians are particularly suited and eager to teach the mechanism to modern students. (We explain this process later in the chapter.) The Austrian attention to the categories of direct versus indirect exchange, and the special case of money, is also attributable to the Austrian focus on market *processes*, rather than the calculation of equilibrium *states* or *positions*. Whatever the reason, it is undeniable that if you read the excerpts from Murray Rothbard assigned for this lesson, you will see a much more thorough discussion of the limitations of direct exchange (and barter) than you will in any standard textbook.

The Advantages of Indirect Exchange

For students who have difficulty keeping long chains of reasoning crisp in their minds, you will probably want to have them draw out the important elements of the narrative involving the farmer seeking shoe repair. The exercise will be useful not only for this lesson, but also later on in Lesson 15 when we discuss the problems of central planning. The students need to get an idea of just how *complex* a modern economy is, and the act of drawing out the sequence of trades necessary to achieve shoe repair might help toward this goal.

To avoid confusion, you should reinforce the text's clarification that the table listing the preferences for the Cobbler, Farmer, and Butcher has simplified the narrative in the body of the text. Specifically, the table omits the Fisherman, because a scenario involving three people was already complicated enough.

Also, some students may not understand the connection between the Cobbler's leisure and the Farmer's repaired shoes. Obviously for a service (such as shoe repair), the seller is giving up leisure, while the buyer is receiving the product or service. In other words, when it comes to the possible gains from trade when one of the items is a service, the seller sacrifices leisure but the buyer isn't gaining the other person's leisure.

The Advantages of Money

To recapitulate the layout of this chapter: First we showed the severe limitations of an economy limited to direct exchange. In the previous section, we relaxed that harsh assumption and allowed for people to engage in indirect exchange.

However, there are still problems with generic indirect exchange, in which people accept things in trade that they intend to trade away in the near future, but where there is no single medium of exchange that just about everyone treats this way. In other words, we are here focusing on the limitations of a world in which some people accept fish, butter, and bacon in indirect exchanges, but other people don't. Those other people might only accept salt, milk, and tobacco in indirect exchanges, which the first group of people would never accept in trade (save for their possible direct desire to use these goods personally in their own households).

When there is no "common denominator" in exchanges—meaning when there isn't a single good that participates on one side of just about all transactions—then it is much more difficult for people to keep track of "the market" and calculate whether they are being offered a good price in a potential trade. The use of money greatly simplifies the computations required. (One of the Suggested Activities expands on this point.)

Who Invented Money?

The idea of **spontaneous order** is quite popular in some academic circles. In order to help the student grasp the concept as it applies to the development of money, you may want to introduce it in more familiar contexts, such as spoken languages or the natural sciences. (One of the Suggested Activities elaborates.) The crucial concept is that there are practices and institutions that are clearly not "natural," in the sense that they were created by human beings, but at the same time their whole scope wasn't consciously designed by any one person or group of people. Too often in political debates, people just assume that a complex social institution must have been deliberately designed by someone, or at least that "experts" could improve on something (the distribution of goods, for example) if they tinker with it.

We emphasize it in the text, but be sure the student realizes that there is nothing that requires gold and/or silver to be money. It is simply the case that in a true free market under modern conditions, people would probably gravitate toward these commodities which would blossom once again into worldwide monetary goods, just as they did in the past.

●●●●●●●●●●●●●●●●●●●●●●●●●●

STUDY QUESTIONS

1. What's the difference between direct and indirect exchange?

In direct exchange, both parties plan on using (either for consumption or production) the item they obtain through the trade. In indirect exchange, at least one of the parties plans on trading away the item obtained through the trade.

2. Why would specialization be impractical in a world limited to direct exchange?

A world limited to direct exchange would require a "double coincidence of wants" before a trade could occur. It would be impractical for someone to specialize in the production of services or goods that were of high value but rarely needed, such as (say) a heart surgeon or an orthodontist. In order to obtain enough food, clothing, and other goods for a comfortable living, the orthodontist would need to find—every week!— someone with meat, bread, etc., who needed work done on his braces, etc. In such a world, people would have to always be ready to fall back on their own production for necessities, and couldn't spend time becoming a true expert in a specialty. Note also that the orthodontist wouldn't be able to accept, say, 100 chickens from a farmer in exchange for a lot of dental work, because if the orthodontist then used some of the chickens to obtain other items, it would no longer be direct exchange. (At least some of the chickens would have served as a medium of exchange for the orthodontist.)

3. How does indirect exchange facilitate the strategy of "one step back, two steps forward"?

With the possibility of indirect exchange, an individual can "sell" her wares and receive something she doesn't directly desire, and in this sense has taken a step back in the goals she can satisfy with her possessions. But if she can then trade away the medium of exchange to obtain something she likes even better than the original possession, she has taken two steps forward.

4. What are the disadvantages of indirect exchange without money?

Without money, various goods all trade against each other directly. This makes it very difficult for someone to determine the "best deal" when he wants to unload a particular good and buy something else. He can quickly spot one way of doing so, but it's a very complicated problem to figure out if there is a more lucrative way. (One of the Suggested Activities elaborates on this idea.)

5. *Describe a society in which the people practice indirect exchange, but have not yet developed money.

If there is indirect exchange, it means that at least some people in the society accept goods that they don't directly want (for production or consumption). So there are media of exchange. However, if money has not yet developed, it means that there is no one medium of exchange that everyone is willing to accept. In other words, some members of the community accept Medium of Exchange #1, while some others accept Medium of Exchange #2, and so forth. In a monetary economy, (virtually) everyone accepts the same medium of exchange.

Supplemental Materials

- Doug French, "Money..." video at **http://mises.org/media/4286.**

  French's talk is aimed at high school students and provides a very understandable introduction to the Austrian view of money. He shows exhibits of different types of money that should interest students.

- Robert Murphy, "The Origin of Money and Its Value," at **http://mises.org/daily/1333.**

  This should be a fairly straightforward article that formally lays out the Austrian view of money. It is unavoidably technical at points because its purpose is to explain the specific contributions of Carl Menger and Ludwig von Mises to economic theory. However, most students should be able to absorb at least the main lessons.

- Gene Callahan, *Economics for Real People*, Chapter 5.

  Callahan covers much of the same territory that we have in our treatment. He opens the discussion with a list of attributes that money typically possesses, such as ease of transport and divisibility. Be aware that these are not requirements for something to qualify as money. Something is money if it is a (nearly) universally accepted medium of exchange. The attributes Callahan discusses are factors that propel certain goods into meeting the definition of money.

- Murray Rothbard, *Man, Economy, and State*, pp. 187–98.

  The Rothbard excerpt analyzes the difference between direct and indirect exchange a bit more formally.

- George Selgin, "The Private Supply of Money," video at **http:// mises.org/media/3037.**

  Much of Selgin's discussion is unnecessary for the basic points of this lesson, but some students may find his historical accounts fascinating. The overwhelming majority simply assume that governments "had" to create money, but Selgin shows the historical superiority of private mints over their government counterparts.

- TIME article from 1933 discussing FDR's gold confiscation, at **http://www.time.com/time/magazine/ article/0,9171,882486-1,00.html.**

  Almost immediately after his inauguration in the depths of the Great Depression, Franklin Delano Roosevelt ordered American citizens to turn in all of their gold (except for rare coins, jewelry, and other non-monetary items). Students may be surprised to learn that before FDR's confiscation, the government was contractually bound to hand over a certain weight of gold to anyone who presented it with U.S. dollars. (Specifically, $20.67 legally entitled the bearer to one gold ounce.) It was because of its historical link to gold that so many people used U.S. paper dollars in the first place.

- R.A. Radford, "The Economic Organization of a P.O.W. Camp," *Economica* vol. 12, 1945, available at **http://www.albany. edu/~mirer/eco110/pow.html.**

  The Radford paper is a classic among economists. Some of it is a bit formal, but most students should still be able to glean the general message. Radford was a P.O.W. during World War II, and in this paper he explains how cigarettes spontaneously evolved into money among the prisoners.

SUGGESTED ACTIVITIES

(1) If appropriate for the student, draw up (or have the student do so) a simulated economy on a sheet of paper, listing 5 – 10 different people and their offer prices for 3 – 5 different commodities. (You should start on the low end of these ranges and then increase them, to see how quickly the complexity increases.) For example you might initially try something like the following:

Alice	Bob	Charlie	Dan	Ed	Frank
10 eggs for 1 pound of bacon	0 eggs for 1 apple	8 eggs for 1 pound of bacon	2 apples for 1 egg	1 egg for 2 apples	0 apples for 1 egg
5 apples for 1 pound of bacon	1 pound of bacon for 50 apples	22 apples for 1 pound of bacon	1 pound of bacon for 12 eggs	1 pound of bacon for 30 apples	1 pound of bacon for 11 eggs

In the context of the above community, ask the student to find the way to achieve the most eggs, starting with a pound of bacon. If limited to direct exchange, the answer would be obvious: Only Alice and Charlie are willing to offer eggs for bacon, and Alice's offer is better. So clearly—if limited to direct exchange—the student should trade with Alice and achieve 10 eggs for a pound of bacon.

However, with the possibility of indirect exchange, things are not so simple. The student needs to check if there is an indirect way to achieve more than 10 eggs, starting with an initial pound of bacon. (Note that we assume that Alice, Bob, etc., will trade as many units as the student wants, at the posted price ratios.) For example, if the student trades with Charlie, he or she can obtain 22 apples for the original pound of bacon. Then the student can take those 22 apples to Ed and obtain 11 eggs. Disregarding the extra hassle, this indirect route yields 11 eggs for the original pound of bacon, versus the 10 eggs using only direct exchange.

With only 5 other people and three commodities total, it's not too difficult to go through and quickly calculate the most advantageous trading paths, for a specified starting number of units of one good and a desired end good. But by introducing more goods and people, the process becomes very difficult very quickly. The point with these exercises isn't even for the student to find the correct answer, but just to see how difficult it becomes without money.

Once you have pushed the student as far as you plan in terms of the complexity of scenarios like the table above, introduce silver money and show how quickly the student can find the best way to transform a pound of bacon into eggs. (Note in the following table, the economy is not necessarily equivalent to the economy depicted in the above table; we are keeping things similar just to show the difference that having a single medium of exchange makes.)

Alice	Bob	Charlie	Dan	Ed	Frank
1 ounce of silver for 1 pound of bacon	1 oz. of silver for 100 apples	1 oz. of silver for ½ pound of bacon	1 ounce of silver for 10 eggs	1 ounce of silver for 8 apples	1 oz. of silver for 2 pounds of bacon
5 apples for 1 ounce of silver	1/10 pound of bacon for 1 ounce of silver	7 apples for 1 ounce of silver	8 eggs for 1 ounce of silver	1/3 pound of bacon for 1 ounce of silver	1 egg for 1 ounce of silver

Using the above table, the first move is easy enough: The student should sell his or her pound of bacon to Charlie, in order to receive 2 oz. of silver. Because all transactions work "through" silver—in other words, nobody is trying to buy bacon with anything other than silver—the student obviously puts him or herself in the most advantageous position by selling the bacon to the person who offers the most silver for it, namely Charlie.

Notice that already, the monetary economy has simplified things for the student. With the previous table, the student wasn't sure which good to trade against in the first round, whereas it is obvious when everyone sells everything for the money commodity.

We have chosen the numbers in the table featuring silver, such that the optimal second step is the "obvious" one of using the 2 ounces of silver to buy 16 eggs from Dan. Looking at the various offers of eggs per unit of silver, clearly Dan offers the best terms.

However, there is a subtlety that you should point out to the advanced student. Strictly speaking, after the student has acquired his or her 2 ounces of silver from Charlie, the next step would be to check for any arbitrage opportunities. This would occur if there were a "guaranteed" way to make money (i.e., silver) by taking advantage of price discrepancies between buyers and sellers. For example, look at the highlighted number 5 for Alice. If Alice were instead willing to sell 12 apples for an ounce of silver, there would be an arbitrage opportunity. The student could take the 2 ounces of silver (obtained from selling the bacon to Charlie), buy 24 apples from Alice, and then sell them to Ed for 3 total ounces of silver. Thus, the student would have transformed the original 2 silver ounces into 3 ounces. The source of this gain would be the student's observation that Alice is selling apples at a price of 1/12 an ounce of silver each, whereas Ed is buying apples at a price of 1/8 per oz. of silver each. Since 1/12 < 1/8, the difference in prices offers a clear speculative opportunity to "buy low, sell high."

To be clear, there are no arbitrage opportunities in the table above; we are simply showing what would happen if the highlighted 5 had instead been a 12. It is easy to check for arbitrage opportunities; the student can look to see if any of the commodities (bacon, eggs, and apples) are being sold on the bottom row for a lower unit price than they are being purchased along the top row. Because of the way fractions work, this is equivalent to checking that the number of units of a good (apples, eggs, or pounds of bacon) is lower in the bottom row, than it is in the top row. For example, to check that there are no arbitrage opportunities in apple investment, the student just needs to verify that the 5 apples and 7 apples on the bottom row (in Alice and Charlie's columns) are lower numbers than the 100 apples and 8 apples in the top row (in Bob and Ed's columns).

Although there is always the possibility of arbitrage—buying low and selling high for a virtually "riskless" gain—speculators are much more likely to spot such opportunities and eliminate them in a monetary economy. Just as it is straightforward for the student to check for such opportunities, so too could Alice, Bob, etc., look around and see if there were easy ways to make silver in this fashion.

In summary, not only does the use of money greatly simplify the first step for a trader—he or she knows to sell wares to the person offering the most units of the money good—but the use of money also makes it easier to see if there is a speculative opportunity because of the pricing among others in the community. Furthermore, in practice average buyers and sellers wouldn't even need to worry about such possibilities, because savvy speculators would most likely have already spotted the arbitrage opportunity and whittled it away through buying and selling.

(To see how this works, consider that if Alice initially were willing to give up 12 apples for an ounce of silver, while Ed gave an ounce of silver for 8 apples, then traders would make a silver gain by buying apples from Alice and selling them to Ed. In principle, a speculator would want to carry out this operation an infinite number of times. But in reality, of course, eventually Alice would run low on apples, and would be overflowing with silver. Ed, on the other hand, would run low on silver and would be overflowing with apples. So the arbitrage opportunity couldn't last forever; eventually Alice would lower the number of apples she offered for an ounce of silver, while Ed would raise the number of apples he required before giving up an ounce of silver.)

(2) Motivate the concept of spontaneous order by discussing more familiar examples. For instance, ask the student "who decides" on the definition of the word *red*. If the student says, "The people who write dictionaries," then ask what would happen if all of the new dictionaries next year defined red as the typical color of ocean water. Would everyone start saying the ocean is red, or would everyone instead say, "The dictionary writers put the wrong definition in for *red!*"? You can also ask, "Which group of people is in charge of physics, or of women's fashion this season?" Of course there are particular people at any moment who have far more influence than others, but it's worth exploring exactly how they *achieved* this position. The goal is for the student to see that these clearly human "things"—the definitions of words in the English language, the current state of the field of physics, or what's "in" for women's fashion this season—aren't the result of a conscious plan created by a single group of experts. These "things" are the result of human action, but not (totally) of human design. Much of the resulting patterns were not anticipated by anybody, and it involved the interaction of millions of people.

Short Answer:
On the lines provided, answer the questions in 1 to 3 sentences.

1. Explain the advantages and limitations of direct exchange.

_____

_____

_____

_____

_____

_____

_____

_____

2. Explain how a community could use indirect exchange but not have money.

_____

_____

_____

_____

_____

_____

_____

_____

3. Explain what economist Friedrich Hayek meant when he used the term "spontaneous order" in reference to the origin of money.

_____

_____

_____

_____

_____

_____

_____

_____

_____

_____

_____

_____

_____

_____

_____

_____

_____

_____

_____

_____

_____

Listing: For each commodity, list the attributes (you can put more than one) of a good money that each has.

     A. Very durable
     B. Easily divisible
     C. Easily transportable
     D. Convenient market value (by weight)
     E. Units very similar quality

4. _____ House

5 _____ Horse

6. _____ Bananas

7. _____ Gold

8. _____ Silver

9. _____ Aluminum

10. _____ Plutonium

11. _____ Emeralds

Short Answer:

1. Explain the advantages and limitations of direct exchange.

SAMPLE FULL CREDIT ANSWER

The advantage of direct exchange is that it allows people to make mutually beneficial trades, so that each person winds up better off. The limitation is that a person looking to make a trade needs to find someone else who desires what the first person is offering, and who also has what the first person wants. This requirement prevents many beneficial trades that involve more than two people.

SAMPLE PARTIAL CREDIT ANSWER

The problem with direct exchange is that a dentist who is hungry has to find a farmer who has a toothache.

SAMPLE NO CREDIT ANSWER

If people directly grow their own food or make their own clothes, they are very limited. It is better to exchange with others.

2. Explain how a community could use indirect exchange but not have money.

SAMPLE FULL CREDIT ANSWER

So long as some people in the community accept items in trade that they intend to trade away in the future, then the community uses indirect exchange. However, if it so happens that no single commodity is accepted as a medium of exchange by everybody in the community, then there wouldn't be a money. In other words, even though lots of people might accept objects intending to trade them away again, the people use different objects in this way.

SAMPLE PARTIAL CREDIT ANSWER

When someone visits another country, his money isn't accepted and he doesn't think what they use is "money" either. But the people in that country aren't using barter.

125

SAMPLE NO CREDIT ANSWER
The people in a community might just use credit cards and checks, without actually carrying money in their wallets.

3. Explain what economist Friedrich Hayek meant when he used the term "spontaneous order" in reference to the origin of money.

SAMPLE FULL CREDIT ANSWER
Hayek meant that nobody planned the creation of money; it just happened naturally as the outgrowth of individuals trying to better themselves. Even so, money is a very useful institution that allows modern economies to work.

SAMPLE PARTIAL CREDIT ANSWER
Hayek meant that nobody invented money.

SAMPLE NO CREDIT ANSWER
Hayek meant that money was created because officials ordered it.

Listing:
For each commodity, list the attributes (you can put more than one) of a good money that each has.

A. Very durable
B. Easily divisible
C. Easily transportable
D. Convenient market value (by weight)
E. Units very similar quality (homogeneous)

[NOTE TO TEACHER: In this section there is some leeway because the classifications are somewhat subjective, though the "correct" answers should be clear from re-reading the discussion at the end of the chapter. We have also included a fifth criterion, homogeneity of units, which simply means that the units of the commodity are basically interchangeable. This is an important trait of a good money that we didn't discuss in the student text.]

4. House   A

5. Horse   C?

6. Bananas   C

7. Gold   A, B, C, D, E

8. Silver   A, B, C, D, E

9. Aluminum   A, B, C, E

10. Plutonium A, B?, E

11. Emeralds   A, C, D

The Division of Labor
and Specialization

The Division of Labor and Specialization

The material on the division of labor and specialization is fairly standard. One difference is tying the concepts to the use of money. Because most textbooks don't dwell much on a monetary vs. a barter economy in the first place, they typically don't explain that money allows a much greater development of the division of labor.

It is a fairly basic point, but be sure the student sees the connection between labor productivity and the standard of living. The only way everyone can continue to *consume* more stuff over time, is if everyone *produces* more stuff over time.

Why Specialization Makes Labor More Productive

For the basic student, the important message of this section is simply that specialization makes labor more productive. For most students, this lesson can best be illustrated by imagining a catastrophe in which most of the world's population is wiped out. Besides feelings of loneliness and despair, the survivors would be in dire straits from a purely materialistic viewpoint as well. Make sure the student understands that this thought experiment illustrates the tremendous advantages of the division of labor.

The more advanced student will benefit from trying to break down the general superiority of specialization into specific causes. (Note that we are using the terms *division of labor* and *specialization* interchangeably, but some writers might make a subtle distinction in which *specialization* is a special case of the division of labor, where people remain in one or a few niche areas. In general, we could imagine a division of labor in which everyone rotates jobs every day or week, so that it wouldn't necessarily be a case of "specialization.")

Enriching Everyone By Focusing on Comparative Advantage

Our earlier concentration on property rights and exchange shows up in this section, as we mention that the benefits of specialization can only be reaped when people are secure in their property and can trade with each other.

The principles of **absolute** and **comparative advantage** are bedrock in modern economics. In this course, we introduce them in a simpler setting (namely a clothing store in the mall) and defer the more traditional treatment—in the context of international trade—until Lesson 19.

Historically, Adam Smith made a very strong case for free trade (in his *Wealth of Nations* in 1776) but the argument relied on absolute advantage. In other words, Smith showed that if England could produce more mutton per hour of (English) labor than France could produce per hour of (French) labor, while at the same time France could produce more wine of a certain quality per hour of labor than England could, then it would make both countries richer if their governments allowed

England to export mutton and import wine from France. This is common sense once we spell out the situation.

However, later economists (such as James Mill and David Ricardo) took the case further and showed that two nations could become wealthier through trade, even if one of them had the absolute advantage in both goods. The country with the absolute advantage in both goods can still benefit by focusing on producing (and exporting some of) the item in which it has the relative, or comparative, advantage. In Lesson 19 we will give a numerical example to illustrate the idea, but for now you should at least understand the historical context of these terms.

For this lesson, you simply need to make sure the student understands that Marcia is better at both tasks. So it's not as obvious at first why Marcia would benefit from hiring John, when she herself could do the job more quickly (and probably better!) than John can. It's obvious why a skilled dentist and a skilled lawyer benefit from trading with each other, but it's not so clear in our example of Marcia and John. The reason, of course, is that Marcia can focus her efforts on what she's *really* good at, by outsourcing the mundane work to John.

STUDY QUESTIONS

[handwritten: Define specialization = each person works on 1 or a few tasks]

1. **What's the connection between specialization and the productivity of labor?**

[handwritten: people can produce more when they specialize]

Specialization greatly increases the productivity of labor.

[handwritten: Productivity of labor = amt of output a worker can produce]

2. ***If the world were filled with identical people, would specialization still be useful?**

[handwritten: eg - Tree removal service w/ dingo + chipper]

Yes, because (among other reasons) people would still have access to different climates and raw materials, and also because initially identical people will develop different skills over time if they specialize in different occupations.

[handwritten: Compare natural vs acquired aptitude (sports) - Calibrating special equipment]

3. **Why is trade important for the division of labor?**

The division of labor only works when people produce more than what they personally will use, and then trade their excess or surplus with others. It does no good to produce ten times as many oranges and steaks, if the farmer has to eat only oranges and the butcher can only eat steak.

[handwritten: Explain absolute advantage = a person can produce more units/hr compared to someone else]
[handwritten: comparative advantage = a person has a relative superiority in a particular task →]

4. ***Explain this statement: "The gains from trade in a case of absolute advantage are obvious, but they can be quite subtle in a case of comparative advantage."**

If Joe is an expert lawyer while Sally is an expert dentist, it is perfectly obvious that they benefit from Joe trading legal services in exchange for Sally's dental work. But in the text's hypothetical case of Marcia the storekeeper and John the hired help, it's not clear at first why Marcia benefits from hiring someone to do a job she could more quickly herself.

[handwritten: eg - heart surgeon can also sweep the floor in the operating room better]

5. **Why is Marcia the storekeeper willing to pay up to $40 to have someone clean her store at the end of the day?**

If Marcia has to clean the store herself, she sacrifices 30 minutes that she could have spent pushing sales. Because it takes her an average of 15 minutes to close a sale, that means Marcia loses out on 2 typical sales if she doesn't hire someone to clean for her. Because the text assumes Marcia nets an average of $20 per sale, her 30 minutes is worth $40 to her, and that is the most she would be willing to pay someone else to do her cleaning.

How does specialization make labor more productive?
- less time wasted switching between tasks
- promotes automation

What is economies of scale?
a condition in which output will increase more than proportionally as inputs are increased (eg - apple orchard)

Comparative advantage - a person has a absolute advantage in every area, but specializes in their field that are the greatest

Supplemental Materials

- Leonard Read, "I, Pencil," at **http://www.econlib.org/library/Essays/rdPncl1.html.**

  Read's article is truly one of the most famous economics pieces of all time. It is self-explanatory.

- Robert Murphy, "Superman Needs an Agent," at **http://mises.org/daily/2242.**

  Another self-explanatory piece. Note the Suggested Activity accompanying the Superman article.

- Gene Callahan, *Economics for Real People*, Chapter 7.

  In this chapter Callahan lays out Ludwig von Mises's conception of different economic roles or functions, as distinct from actual people. For example, the economist can contrast "the entrepreneur" with "the worker," without having in mind two specific people and even disregarding the fact that all workers are (part) entrepreneurs because they must make forecasts about future career paths, etc. There are some technical terms from Austrian economics (such as the "evenly rotating economy") that the beginner student can safely ignore.

- Murray Rothbard, *Man, Economy, and State*, pp. 95–102, 213–31.

  For the student who has been reading all the Rothbard selections, the above excerpts will help round out the material. However, Rothbard pursues several technical tangents that are not directly needed to understand the basics of the division of labor. Beginning students can safely skip pages 213–31.

SUGGESTED ACTIVITIES

(1) Have the student keep track of examples of the division of labor during the day, which are not part of someone's paid job. (E.g., the neighbors tending to their yard, with the husband cleaning out the gutters while the wife pulls weeds, as opposed to each spouse pulling half of the weeds and cleaning out half of the gutters.)

(2) Have the student keep track of examples of economies of scale during the day, which are not part of someone's paid job. (E.g., someone running to get fastfood and asking if anyone else wants anything. It doesn't take twice as much effort, gas, etc., in order to bring home two burgers as it takes to bring home one burger.)

(3) Before reading the article from the Supplemental Materials, have the student brainstorm and come up with various jobs that Superman could perform. Try to estimate the job that would yield him the highest income. See how the analysis compares to Murphy's.

Short Answer:
On the lines provided, answer the questions in 1 to 3 sentences.

1. What is the difference between absolute advantage and comparative advantage?

_____

_____

_____

_____

_____

_____

_____

2. Give an example—not from the textbook—involving two people and two lines of production, where one party has the absolute advantage in both lines, but it still obviously makes sense for each to focus on his or her comparative advantage.

_____

_____

_____

_____

_____

_____

_____

_____

3. Identify a profession for which one might require a certain natural aptitude, and explain why.

_____

_____

_____

_____

_____

_____

_____

_____

_____

_____

4. Identify a profession in which current practitioners don't require much of a natural aptitude but where extensive training / experience is necessary.

_____

_____

_____

_____

_____

_____

_____

_____

_____

5. Explain why, in a system with no division of labor, it is likely that most people would be living in or on the edge of poverty.

_____

_____

_____

_____

_____

_____

_____

_____

_____

_____

6. Describe a scenario in which a doubling of inputs more than doubles the output. What do economists call this phenomenon?

_____

_____

_____

_____

_____

_____

_____

_____

_____

Short Answer:

1. What is the difference between absolute advantage and comparative advantage?

SAMPLE FULL CREDIT ANSWER

Absolute advantage means that a person (or country) is better at doing something than another person (or country). For example, one person might be able to make 10 pizzas per hour, while someone else can only make 8. Comparative advantage means that it is efficient for a person (or country) to concentrate in a particular task—whether or not there is an absolute advantage in it—because this outlet offers the best tradeoff with other potential tasks. [NOTE TO TEACHER: These answers will probably be all over the place. What's crucial is that the student understands that absolute advantage refers to the task in isolation, just relying on the numbers. In contrast, comparative advantage can only be determined in the context of all the possible tasks, and it has to do with what is most efficient.]

SAMPLE PARTIAL CREDIT ANSWER

Comparative advantage is when people do the thing they're good at.

SAMPLE NO CREDIT ANSWER

If people have different goods then they gain an advantage by trading.

2. Give an example—not from the textbook—involving two people and two lines of production, where one party has the absolute advantage in both lines, but it still obviously makes sense for each to focus on his or her comparative advantage.

[The pattern here will be finding something "obvious" where one person is better at both things. The student doesn't need to be mathematical in the sense of listing numbers, but ideally the student will understand that absolute advantage does involve numbers. For example, a heart surgeon can probably deliver more newspapers per day than the neighborhood kid, and can successfully operate more times per day, but it makes sense for the kid to deliver all the newspapers so that the heart surgeon can focus on where he or she is really good.]

3. Identify a profession for which one might require a certain natural aptitude, and explain why.

SAMPLE FULL CREDIT ANSWER
Basketball players need to be naturally quick. No matter how much they practice shooting and dribbling, if they have always been really slow, they're not going to be good at basketball.

SAMPLE PARTIAL CREDIT ANSWER
Race car driver.

SAMPLE NO CREDIT ANSWER
Cashier.

4. Identify a profession in which current practitioners don't require much of a natural aptitude but where extensive training / experience is necessary.

SAMPLE FULL CREDIT ANSWER
Teaching English / being manager of a store in the mall / data entry for a particular company's unique database.

[NOTE TO TEACHER: For just about any profession, there is some natural aptitude required, in order to excel. For example, some people just aren't "management material" and could never become the manager of a store in the mall, no matter how long they worked there. But that seems different from saying that some people could never be theoretical physicists, or starting pitchers for the Yankees, no matter how long they prepared. The important thing is that the student understands the difference between natural aptitude and training.]

5. Explain why, in a system with no division of labor, it is likely that most people would be living in or on the edge of poverty.

SAMPLE FULL CREDIT ANSWER
The division of labor greatly enhances the productivity of labor, meaning that more goods are produced per hour of labor. When people specialize and trade, there is more stuff to go around. Without the division of labor, everyone would produce his own food, make his own clothes, etc., and would be extremely poor.

SAMPLE PARTIAL CREDIT ANSWER
People would grow their own food etc.

SAMPLE NO CREDIT ANSWER
People wouldn't have any money if no one bought their stuff.

6. Describe a scenario in which a doubling of inputs more than doubles the output. What do economists call this phenomenon?

SAMPLE FULL CREDIT ANSWER
If I double the amount of time, raw pasta, etc. that I devote to the task, I can more than double the amount of dinner I prepare. That's why it makes sense for people living in a household to take turns making dinner (and for restaurants to open). This phenomenon is called "economies of scale."

SAMPLE PARTIAL CREDIT ANSWER
Raking leaves.

SAMPLE NO CREDIT ANSWER
Sometimes workers might get paid double for overtime.

Entrepreneurship and Competition

Entrepreneurship

Believe it or not, many standard economics textbooks do not even mention the role of entrepreneurs, let alone describe them as the "driving force" of a market economy. Ludwig von Mises and other members of the Austrian School naturally focus on entrepreneurship as the heart of a market, because Austrians focus on processes rather than equilibrium snapshots. In other words, economists who concentrate on how a market evolves over time will be very interested in the role that entrepreneurship plays.

Strictly speaking, entrepreneurs strive after *psychic* profit. In other words, everyone seeks to improve his or her situation, according to subjective preferences. This applies to Mother Teresa as well as to Henry Paulson. However, at this level it's probably easiest to have students concentrate on the familiar notion of a businessperson trying to "make money." But to remain technically accurate, we use the term monetary profit, and take care not to make sweeping statements to the effect that *all* entrepreneurs seek to generate monetary profits.

Competition Protects Customers

Be sure the student understands the significance of competition in channeling the activities of businesspeople, "keeping them honest." Later on in the course, we will see that the reason socialism and the mixed economy perform so poorly is not that individuals become magically corrupt or evil under those systems. Rather, the same people in a genuine free market will tend to behave in ways that promote social cooperation and harmony, whereas they will exploit their neighbors when placed into a different institutional framework. (One of the Suggested Activities follows up on this.)

Competition Protects Workers

In this section we have used phrases such as "fair price" and "overpay." Please be sure that the student understands the limited scope of these terms. As we explain in the footnotes, all transactions in a pure market economy are fair, in the sense that they are voluntary exchanges of property. The point is that competition promotes outcomes that most people have in mind when they desire that economic activities be "fair." In other words, people who initially think that the government needs to protect consumers and workers from greedy businesspeople, probably don't understand how markets actually work.

Depending on the student, you will have to decide how deeply to push the analysis of labor productivity and wage payments. There is an extensive treatment in Rothbard, but it goes far beyond what the basic student requires. The one thing you should stress to all students, however, is that *all* resource owners receive payments based on these principles. In other words, the owner of, say, a parcel of land or a snowblower, can rent these out to businesses at prices determined by the marginal product of those resources. We have focused on an example involving labor services just because this is probably the most interesting and relevant to the student.

S T U D Y   Q U E S T I O N S

Define entrepreneur – produces goods/services, hires workers, buys resources

1. Why is the entrepreneur the "driving force" of a market economy?

It is the entrepreneur who directly organizes economic affairs, deciding how resources will be combined and which goods will be produced in what quantities.

Define
revenue
expense
profit
loss

what is a capitalist?

2. *In the real world, why are all capitalists also entrepreneurs?

In textbooks we neatly isolate the various functions (entrepreneur, capitalist, laborer, landowner, etc.). However in reality, an entrepreneur is ultimately someone who surveys the status quo and takes risky or uncertain actions to strive for a better future. Specifically, anyone who invests in a venture is acting as an entrepreneur, because the capitalist must believe in the project and stands to lose everything if the forecast is wrong.

3. What motivates and regulates entrepreneurs in a market economy?

Competition.

4. How does the competitive process unfold through "imitation and innovation"?

No entrepreneur starts from scratch. He or she first sees what others are doing, and then tries to make improvements in order to attract customers from others. Even someone who starts a completely new business is still competing (ultimately) against all other entrepreneurs, for the scarce dollars of potential customers. For example, a movie theater owner competes not merely with other theater owners, but also with the owners of amusement parks, and even the owners of restaurants and gyms. Whenever a customer spends money at one business, that is less money available for other shops.

5. How does competition protect workers?

If a particular worker is being paid less than his or her marginal product, there is an opportunity for a competing entrepreneur to offer a higher wage and pocket the (smaller) gap. The only logical stopping point for this process is when all workers are paid in line with how much they contribute.

Supplemental Materials

- Jeffrey Tucker, "Technology and Social Change," video at **http:// mises.org/MediaPlayer.aspx?Id=4990**.

    Tucker's talk is aimed at high school students and provides a very good introduction to the idea of competition as "imitation and innovation."

- R.W. Grant, "Tom Smith and His Incredible Bread Machine," at **http://www.youtube.com/watch?v=ycGRERrGsMo**.

    This simple tale should illustrate the basic ideas behind the fairness of the competitive process and letting producers keep the fruits of their labors.

- Dom Armentano, "The Anatomy of Antitrust," an interview in *The Austrian Economics Newsletter* at **http://mises.org/ journals/aen/aen398.asp**.

    For more advanced students, the discussion of competition naturally includes the mainstream economic notions of "perfect competition" and monopoly. In this course we will not develop these topics because beginning students often find it difficult to learn a framework only to have it knocked down. Since we think the mainstream understanding of competition in very misleading, we do not discuss it in the main text. However, advanced students should look to the Armentano, DiLorenzo, and Rothbard discussions to relate this chapter to more typical treatments.

- Thomas DiLorenzo, "Competition and Monopoly," video at **http://mises.org/media/4356**.

    A good introduction to the Austrian vs. the mainstream economics view of competition.

- Thomas Woods, "Myths and Facts About Big Business," audio at **http://mises.org/media/1887.**

  Woods's discussion shows that much of the modern understanding of the evils of unregulated big business is actually due to faulty history. Contrary to popular belief, the "robber barons"—to the extent that they operated in the market, rather than getting privileges from the government—actually served their customers with higher quality and lower prices.

- Ludwig von Mises, *Human Action*, pp. 270–79.

  In this excerpt Mises discusses the idea of "consumer sovereignty," in which competition and the desire for profits causes entrepreneurs to obey the wishes of the consumers. The basic idea is that even though the owners of big businesses seem to be "in charge" to a superficial observer of capitalism, in reality the "titans" of business ultimately answer to the customer, the true boss. This is a crucial aspect of Mises's overall view of capitalism.

- Murray Rothbard, *Man, Economy, and State*, pp. 509–16, 636–75. (**)

  We have placed two asterisks after the above excerpts, because these selections from Rothbard can be quite technical. We are only recommending them for the advanced student who wants to read a sample of an Austrian critique of mainstream monopoly theory. Even the first excerpt, which focuses on entrepreneurship, is filled with jargon such as DMVP (discounted marginal value product) and ERE (evenly rotating economy) which would only fully make sense for a student who has read earlier sections of the treatise.

SUGGESTED ACTIVITIES

(1) Have the student identify examples where competition regulates behavior. For example, if one grocery store begins offering carts designed as racecars (for little kids to use while their parents shop), then others usually follow suit. Or perhaps the student knows a particular teenager who is quite rude in personal affairs, but is a model of courtesy when working as a waiter at a country club. (In this case, the student could explain that the waiter is competing against other waiters for tips—in other words, the diners will judge his performance based on how it stacks up with other waiters' performances—or the student could say that the waiter is part of the whole restaurant's effort to compete against other businesses for the customer's dollars.) There are also examples that are not so obviously tied to markets, for example athletes lifting weights and watching their diets in preparation for a sports season, or boys and girls buying expensive clothes and otherwise grooming themselves in an effort to compete for the most attractive dates.

(2) Discuss "outrageous" salaries with the student, such as those earned by star athletes and movie stars. Regardless of the ultimate ethical judgment, be sure the student understands that these salaries are the result of marginal productivity. For example, if a movie producer adds George Clooney to the cast of a movie that originally has no other household names, this decision will almost certainly allow the producer to earn millions of dollars more in revenue from the film. That is why Clooney can command such a high salary. If the student thinks "no one needs to make that much," ask what the alternative should be. For example, if Clooney's presence increases box office revenues by $3 million, but Clooney is limited to a "reasonable" $500,000 paycheck, then does the movie studio get to pocket the difference?

Matching Essential Terminology:
Write the appropriate term on the line beside its description.

Entrepreneur   Revenues   Expenses   Profit   Competition

1. _____ Protects the interests of both consumers and workers.

2. _____ The money earned from customers in exchange for products and services.

3. _____ Revenues minus expenses.

4. _____ Anyone who starts a new business or develops a new product.

5. _____ The money a business pays to workers, suppliers, landlords, etc.

Short Answer:
On the lines provided, answer the questions in 1 to 3 sentences.

6. Explain how entrepreneurs are the driving force of a market economy.

_____

_____

_____

_____

_____

_____

7. Explain how an employer calculates the marginal productivity of a worker.

_____

_____

_____

_____

_____

_____

_____

_____

_____

_____

8. Explain how competition protects workers. *from arbitrarily low wages*

_____

_____

_____

_____

_____

_____

_____

_____

_____

9. Explain how competition protects consumers. *from arbitary high prices*

_____

_____

_____

_____

_____

_____

_____

_____

_____

_____

~~How~~ What Keeps entrepreneurs honest?

Matching Essential Terminology:

1. Competition

2. Revenues

3. Profit

4. Entrepreneur

5. Expenses

Short Answer:

6. Explain how entrepreneurs are the driving force of a market economy.

SAMPLE FULL CREDIT ANSWER
Entrepreneurs perceive an opportunity to hire workers and buy other resources, in order to create a product or service for consumers. If the entrepreneurs are successful, they earn a profit, meaning that (in a sense) they are transforming resources into finished goods/services that have a higher value than what was used up in making them. It is the entrepreneurs who make the day-to-day decisions on how resources will be used.

SAMPLE PARTIAL CREDIT ANSWER
Entrepreneurs start new businesses.

SAMPLE NO CREDIT ANSWER
Under communism, the government can tell workers what jobs they must perform, whereas the entrepreneurs do this under capitalism.

7. Explain how an employer calculates the marginal productivity of a worker.

SAMPLE FULL CREDIT ANSWER
The employer estimates how much income or profit he would earn with the worker, compared to how much he would earn without the worker. (These estimates don't count the additional expense of hiring the worker.) The difference is the marginal productivity of the worker, and represents the most that the employer would pay to hire her.

SAMPLE PARTIAL CREDIT ANSWER
The employer pays the worker how much she is worth to the company.

SAMPLE NO CREDIT ANSWER
The employer has to pay enough to get the worker to accept the job.

8. Explain how competition protects workers.

SAMPLE FULL CREDIT ANSWER
If a worker isn't being paid his marginal product, there is a "gap" making it worthwhile for a rival employer to make a better offer. In the long run, we therefore expect workers to make (close to) their marginal products.

SAMPLE PARTIAL CREDIT ANSWER
A worker can always quit her job if she doesn't like it.

SAMPLE NO CREDIT ANSWER
In a free market, the employer was a worker once too, and so remembers what it was like.

9. Explain how competition protects consumers.

SAMPLE FULL CREDIT ANSWER

If a firm is making a low-quality or high-priced product, a rival firm can capture market share by offering higher-quality and/or lower-priced items. No business can force consumers to buy its products or services.

SAMPLE PARTIAL CREDIT ANSWER

Consumers can shop around.

SAMPLE NO CREDIT ANSWER

Even in capitalist countries, there are regulations on basic safety standards etc., to make sure no one is selling hazardous goods.

Income, Saving, and Investment

Income, Saving, and Investment

I n terms of practical life lessons, this chapter is one of the most important in the book. Be sure the student really understands the power of compound interest, and that even people with modest paychecks can become millionaires if they begin saving early in their career.

Note that the possibly unfamiliar term **dissaving** refers to someone who lives above his means—in other words, consumes more than his income—but doesn't borrow from outside lenders. Rather, the person finances his extra consumption by drawing down previously accumulated savings.

Investment Increases Future Income

The tables should be self-explanatory to you, but make sure the student understands how all the numbers fit together. A very useful exercise (or test question) could involve your own table (with some of the numbers altered) and a few of the cells left blank. With a calculator or even just pencil and paper, the student should be able to fill in the missing cells.

Retirement

Depending on your own views, you may want to tie in the discussion of saving for retirement with a broader discussion of the importance of thrift and self-reliance. In other words, one doesn't need to become a financial burden on the next generation if he or she has adequately saved during the prime working years. (More sophisticated students should learn about life and health insurance policies as well.)

How Saving and Investment Increase An Economy's Future Output

In order to understand the business cycle theory presented in Lesson 23, it's necessary for the student to understand how genuine savings and investment fuel an advancing economy. In other words, the student should first learn how things can go right (a sustainable expansion in the economy) before learning how they go wrong (an unsustainable boom period followed by an inevitable bust or recession).

These issues will be covered in greater depth in the Advanced Lessons 12 – 14, but for now make sure the student understands two central ideas: First, the growing wealth of a saver is not automatically "canceled out" by the growing indebtedness of a borrower. Specifically, what can happen is that the borrower (which can be a business firm) uses loaned funds to expand production. So although it's true that a growing corporation (for example) must take on debt if it wants to borrow money to finance a new plant, the action is not really comparable to an individual placing a trip to Tahiti on his personal credit card. The new factory allows the business to produce and sell more, earning higher revenues with which to finance the interest payments on its higher debt.

The second important idea in this section is that the student sees the _physical_ underpinnings of economic growth through saving and investment. In other words, people aren't simply wealthier because their bank balances rise exponentially over time earning interest. Just as Robinson Crusoe's standard of living went up because of saving and investment (in a pole, etc.), so too does a modern economy grow richer when its output is focused more on capital goods and less on consumption goods.

As a final caution, note that we are deliberately sidestepping the issue of adjustment to a new configuration of spending. A Keynesian economist would worry that a sudden and unexpected increase in saving by most people in the community would lead to a recession. Some of the Supplemental readings address these issues, but in the main text we wanted to stick to the basic point that financial saving and investment has a corresponding "real" component, in terms of the shift in capital/consumer goods mix of output.

Key Pts: ① Interest allows one to save + invest now, in order to increase income in the future.

② Economy is physically transformed when people save & invest.

③ One person's S&I doesn't force someone else to sink into debt

STUDY QUESTIONS

*1

1. Can investment occur without saving?

No. The only way there are resources (whether financial or physical) available for investment, is if someone has lived below his or her means, i.e., saved.

2. What are the pros and cons of saving a high fraction of your income?

The pros are a higher future wealth and income, the cons are less consumption in the *now or* near term.

3. What's the connection between saving and retirement?

People can fund their own retirement lifestyle by saving enough during their working years.

4. If someone borrows in order to buy today rather than waiting to pay cash, is this an example of uneconomical behavior?

No, it simply illustrates the person's preferences. Just as one person might be willing to pay $50 on a juicy steak, while another person would regard this as absurd, so too might someone be willing to pay a high interest rate in order to consume earlier rather than later. There is nothing intrinsically irrational or uneconomical about such a decision, which couldn't be applied just as well to other consumer decisions.

p137 Go over Paul + Freddie

p139 Retirement chart

p 142

5. *Is it possible for every individual in the community to accumulate assets for retirement—or does one person's rising wealth translate into someone else's rising debt?**

Yes, everyone in principle can accumulate financial assets to fund retirement. It's not the case that one person's accumulating wealth translates into someone else's growing indebtedness. (It's true that various corporations and other entities must be on "the other side" of someone else's growing stockpile of financial claims, but this need not reflect a growing danger to the corporations, so long as they are using the loans productively.)

*#1 Income = earnings = revenues - expenses
*#2 Savings = amt by which income > spending
*#3 Investment = savings spent in the hopes of increasing future income

6. Explain what happens savings & investment go toward productive enterprise rather than individual consumption.

Supplemental Materials

• Gene Callahan, *Economics for Real People*, Chapter 8.

> In this chapter Callahan spells out the Austrian view of the structure of production. It is more advanced than our discussion, but should still be quite accessible to most students.

• Robert Murphy, "Cut Taxes for the Right Reasons," at **http:// mises.org/daily/3332.**

> Murphy points out that even many "free market" commentators often fall prey to the same Keynesian fallacies that they think they are debunking. Specifically, tax cuts do indeed promote economic growth, but not because they allow people to "spend more."

• George Reisman, "Economic Recovery Requires Capital Accumulation..." at **http://mises.org/daily/3353.**

> The Reisman article was written in the wake of the housing bust and the various "stimulus" efforts of the Bush and Obama administrations. Students need not read the entire article, but it may be interesting for some because it applies our general lesson to a specific historical situation.

SUGGESTED ACTIVITIES

(1) Using Excel or another spreadsheet application, construct your own table patterned on the text's example of Frugal Freddy and Prodigal Paul. Print out portions of the table, with some of the numbers hidden. Ask the student to fill in the blanks.

(2) Using either a spreadsheet or online calculator (just google "wealth accumulation calculator"), have the student play with the numbers to see how long it would take to achieve a desired target level of wealth. For example, someone who earns $25,000, saves a constant 10% of total income, and earns a tax-free return of 8% annually, would accumulate almost $1 million after 30 years. The point of course is not to encourage greed, but to show the student the surprising power of compound interest—of earning (new) interest on the built-up interest of the past—and what Albert Einstein reportedly referred to as the "most powerful force in the universe."

(3) For the advanced student, discuss the idea that the working generation must support the older (retired) generation. In one sense this is always true; anytime a retired person goes grocery shopping, she's "skimming" food from the harvest of current workers. However, so long as the retired person is living off of previously saved wealth, part of what's happening is that the current workers are more productive because of previous investments by the now-retired person. So the total output of food is greater, because there are more tractors, fertilizer, etc., due to the years of abstinence and accumulation during the now-retired person's working years. For more on this idea (in the context of debates over Social Security), see this article: **http://mises.org/daily/5658/Is-Social-Security-a-Ponzi-Scheme.**

Matching Essential Terminology:
Write the appropriate term on the line beside its description.

Income	Savings	Revenues
Expenses	Borrowing	Investment

1. _____ The difference between income and how much is spent on consumption.

2. _____ Spending intended to generate more income in the future.

3. _____ How much can be spent on consumption today, without impairing future income.

4. _____ A way to consume more than one's income during a certain time period.

Short Answer:
On the lines provided, answer the questions in 1 to 3 sentences.

5. If you expect to live to at least 80 years old, why should you seriously consider saving a large amount of your income and investing it while you are young?

_____

_____

_____

_____

_____

_____

6. Respond to someone who says, "It hurts the economy when people save too much, because if people don't spend, then businesses can't hire workers."

_____

_____

_____

_____

_____

_____

_____

_____

_____

7. How does the accumulation of capital goods help workers who don't own them?

_____

_____

_____

_____

_____

_____

_____

_____

_____

_____

8. Respond to someone who says, "For every lender who grows rich, there must be a borrower who grows poor."

_____

_____

_____

_____

_____

_____

_____

_____

_____

_____

Matching Essential Terminology:

1. Savings

2. Investment

3. Income

4. Borrowing

Short Answer:

5. If you expect to live to at least 80 years old, why should you seriously consider saving a large amount of your income and investing it while you are young?

SAMPLE FULL CREDIT ANSWER
At some point I will not want to, or even be able to, work full time and earn an income. I will want to have a big stockpile of savings to live off of at that point, so that I don't need to ask my family or the government to support me. Because of compound interest, if I start saving just a little bit earlier in my life, it can have a tremendous impact on how much wealth I have when I retire.

SAMPLE PARTIAL CREDIT ANSWER
I need to save so that I will be able to live when I am older.

SAMPLE NO CREDIT ANSWER
If I don't invest then the economy will fall apart.

6. Respond to someone who says, "It hurts the economy when people save too much, because if people don't spend, then businesses can't hire workers."

SAMPLE FULL CREDIT ANSWER
When people save, that allows for more investment which fills the gap in spending. After the economy adjusts to the new level of saving, everybody can still get a job. It's just that more workers will be making things like tools and equipment, rather than restaurant meals and music concerts.

SAMPLE PARTIAL CREDIT ANSWER
The economy will eventually adjust even if people start saving a lot.

SAMPLE NO CREDIT ANSWER
Nobody can actually save 100% of his income, because he would starve to death. So even though it might hurt the economy, it won't be that bad in practice.

7. How does the accumulation of capital goods help workers who don't own them?

SAMPLE FULL CREDIT ANSWER
Workers are paid according to their marginal productivity. When they combine their labor with better tools and equipment, workers can produce more per hour, so they end up earning a higher wage, even if they don't own the tools they're using.

SAMPLE PARTIAL CREDIT ANSWER
If more stuff is produced, people are richer.

SAMPLE NO CREDIT ANSWER
The workers can save up and buy the new tools and eventually this makes them better off too.

8. Respond to someone who says, "For every lender who grows rich, there must be a borrower who grows poor."

SAMPLE FULL CREDIT ANSWER

This is wrong because it overlooks the possibility of "productive borrowing." A business can borrow money by issuing bonds, for example, and use the funds to invest in expanding its operations. Although the business has to pay out interest on the loans, its investment gives it higher revenues, so it can afford to do so and is better off for having borrowed the money.

SAMPLE PARTIAL CREDIT ANSWER

That might be true in some cases but it isn't always true.

SAMPLE NO CREDIT ANSWER

If someone just borrows a little bit, then it might not make him actually poor.

Supply and Demand

Supply and Demand: The Purpose

The material in this lesson is standard. As the text explains, supply and demand graphs are very useful to keep our thoughts organized when we work through the effects of a hypothetical change in the market. Even professional economists often start their basic analysis with some version of a supply and demand graph.

For the advanced student, you should stress that there is not a "theory" of supply and demand. All changes in market prices can be "explained" by reference to movements of supply and demand curves or schedules. It is possible that future economists will abandon the framework in favor of something more convenient, but even if this occurs, it won't be because of some future empirical finding. Rather, future economists might develop an alternative framework that provides a superior understanding of market prices.

Demand: Its Definition and Its Law

It is very important for the student to distinguish demand versus supply, and to be able to analyze them separately. This is the only way the student will be able to correctly answer questions concerning the impact of particular changes in a market.

Make sure the student understands that the demand schedule is a list of *hypothetical* prices and that the schedule applies *at a particular moment in time.* Strictly speaking, we do not "observe" or "catalog" someone's demand schedule by writing down how many gallons of gasoline she buys over the course of several months (with different prices each day). The demand schedule for each person in principle can change from moment to moment.

As a footnote indicates, the Law of Demand is interpreted differently by different economists. Some think that it is a logical deduction from rational action in the face of scarcity, and that any apparent "violations" are really different goods. For example, a woman with a taste for fine jewelry might buy more units of a particular brand when they are more expensive, because if the sale price were too low, the woman would suspect the jewelry to be stolen or fake. But this wouldn't violate the Law of Demand if we insist that people's subjective perception of the good cannot be influenced directly by the price, in order for the law to apply.

Other economists believe that the Law of Demand is merely an empirical regularity, that could in principle be contradicted by the facts. Note that strictly speaking, it would be impossible to truly falsify the Law of Demand, because the underlying preferences (and hence demand schedule) could change in between measurements. For example, if Sally buys 13 gallons of gasoline at $2.50 per gallon on Monday, but she buys 0 gallons on Tuesday even though the price has dropped to $2.45, that is obviously not a violation of the Law of Demand, because on Tuesday Sally is still driving with a nearly full tank of gas. If you understand this simple example, you can see how it would be impossible to ever truly refute the Law of Demand with an experiment.

If the student plans on taking standard economics courses in the future, you should spend some time working with demand (and supply) schedules and graphs, to make sure the student truly understands how they work. However, if this course is the last that the student is likely to take in economics, the ability to translate numerical schedules into graphs is not particularly important. The crucial skill is that the student can use generic supply and demand curves to walk through the impact of a stipulated change in market conditions, in order to identify *the direction* in which price and quantity will move.

Supply: Its Definition and Its Law

Unfortunately the gasoline market is not the best illustration of the Law of Supply, because it may seem a bit contrived as to why producers sell progressively larger quantities at higher prices. (We chose the gasoline market because it is very convenient for illustrating the demand side.)

The Law of Demand is fairly intuitive, but the Law of Supply may not be as obvious. Standard textbooks usually explain rising supply curves as the result of rising cost curves. In other words, at some point it becomes progressively more expensive (per unit) to produce more units of a good, and so producers will need to charge more per unit in order to be willing to operate at larger and larger levels of output. However, we have not dwelt on this issue (even though it's true as far as it goes) because it reinforces the false idea that market prices are caused by costs of production. In reality "costs" are simply *prices* of labor and other resources, and so we haven't really provided a full explanation if we say that market prices are caused by "costs." If you haven't already done so, you might benefit from reading Robert Murphy's discussion of classical versus modern price theory, at **http://mises.org/journals/ jls/20_1/20_1_3.pdf.**

One subtlety that might shed some light on the Law of Supply is that some producers drop out of the market altogether below a certain price point. In other words, even if the student has trouble seeing why a given producer would sell more units at $100 rather than $99—if the producer still earns profit at $99 per unit—the student should be able to understand that producers are not identical, and so some of them might not be able to turn a profit at a price of $99. Of course this analysis too runs the risk of teaching the student the *false* theory that "costs determine prices," so you will have to decide whether to pursue this train of thought.

Using Supply and Demand to Explain the Market Price

Beyond understanding how market forces tend to eliminate shortages and surpluses (or gluts), this material is important because later in the course the student will learn how government price controls lead to *permanent* shortages and gluts.

Using Supply and Demand to Understand Price Changes

The central skill for this lesson is the ability to take a verbal description of a change in a market, and use supply and demand analysis to say which way price and quantity will move. The five examples should be self-explanatory.

The most common pitfall for students in this setting is to confuse a shift in demand (or supply) with a movement along the demand (or supply) curve. College economics professors are often quite adamant on this point, because it is so crucial for clearly thinking through the impacts of a hypothetical change. We encourage you to be mindful of this distinction, and to correct the student if he says, "The price falls and so demand increases," when really he should say, "The price falls and so the *quantity demanded* increases," or, "The price falls and so we move outward on the demand curve."

Remember, the big picture here is that economists are trying to separate out all influences on consumer and producer behavior *except* those directly dealing with the price. So a change in a good's price will never shift the supply or demand curves. (Be careful: The change in the price of one good can shift the supply or demand curves of a *different* good. A change in the price of oranges doesn't affect the supply or demand for oranges; on the contrary, we use the supply and demand curves for oranges to explain the price of oranges! However, a change in the price of oranges can certainly affect the demand for apples, or the supply of orange juice.)

• •

STUDY QUESTIONS

1. Why does the text say that supply and demand can never be proven false?

The concepts of supply and demand are not "theories," they are instead tools of analysis. Future economists might stop using them as tools if they find different ways of explaining market prices that are more convenient or superior in some other fashion.

2. Why does the text say that demand is a snapshot in time?

A person's demand schedule is an instantaneous relationship between *hypothetical* prices and the corresponding quantity the person would buy at each price. If time passes, the person's preferences or other factors might change, leading to a different demand schedule.

3. How do you go from individual demand or supply schedules, to market demand and supply schedules?

At each price, the market quantity of demand or supply is the summation of the individual quantities at that price.

4. Explain how the market process tends to push prices toward their equilibrium levels.

If the price is above the equilibrium level, the quantity supplied exceeds the quantity demanded, meaning there is a surplus or glut. Because producers are trying to sell more units than buyers wish to purchase, they tend to lower their asking price. On the other hand, if the price is below the equilibrium level, the quantity demanded exceeds the quantity supplied, meaning there is a shortage. Because consumers are trying to buy more units than producers wish to sell, producers have an incentive to raise their asking price (or consumers bid higher prices, depending on the mechanics of the particular market).

5. If supply increases while demand decreases, what can we say about the change in (equilibrium) price? What about the change in (equilibrium) quantity?

The equilibrium price will definitely drop, because both changes point in that direction. However, we don't know what will happen to the equilibrium quantity, because the supply shift tends to increase it, while the demand shift tends to decrease it. Without more information we don't know which effect will dominate.

1. Define <u>demand</u> = relationship between the price for a good or service, & the number of units that consumers want to purchase at each hypothethecal price

2. What is the law of demand? Give an example
If other influences stay the same, then a lower price will lead consumers to buy more units of a good or service while a higher price will lead them to buy fewer units.

3. Define supply

Supplemental Materials

- Murray Rothbard, *Man, Economy, and State*, pp. 238–49.

  In this excerpt, Rothbard goes from individual preference rankings to market demand and supply curves. Remember that in Rothbard's exposition, items in parentheses refer to things that the individual does not have in his or her possession.

SUGGESTED ACTIVITIES

(1) Look at the sample test questions for supply and demand graphing exercises. Invent your own to give the student practice.

(2) Have the student read the newspaper or watch the news looking for examples of confusion regarding price movements. (Typically the confusion will occur when the reporter mistakes a shift in the curve for a movement along the curve.)

(3) Have the student take several different industries and explain why producers would exhibit rising supply curves (i.e., obey the Law of Supply). In other words, just as the text gave a specific story to explain the motivations of the three gasoline producers—and why they would sell more units at higher prices—have the student come up with similar explanations for why the producers in other industries might do the same. For example, why would the leaders of Saudi Arabia decide to pump more oil when the price of oil is $100 per barrel rather than $70?

Multiple Choice:
Write the letter of the best answer.

1. Rebecca left for the store hoping to benefit from a huge sale on a particular LCD TV. However, by the time she arrived, a sales clerk informed her that the store had only stocked 10 of that particular TV, and that they sold out of them within twenty minutes. And, of course, there are no rain checks. How should we describe this situation?

    A. glut
    B. shortage
    C. surplus
    D. equilibrium

2. This principle states that lower prices of a good or service tend to make people want either the same or a greater amount of that good or service.

    A. Law of Comparative Advantage
    B. Law of Supply
    C. Law of Demand
    D. Murphy's Law

3. Ryan worked furiously in his studio, sculpting little trolls from manure. However, no matter how little he asked for a price, he could find no buyers. Someone might have told Ryan that there was probably little _____ for manure-based troll sculptures?

    A. supply
    B. equilibrium
    C. cost
    D. demand

4. The Law of Supply says that

    A. a lower price will tend to lead a consumer to buy either the same or a greater amount of the good or service.

    B. consumers want to buy more units of something than producers want to sell at a particular price.

    C. as the market price of a good or service rises, producers tend to offer the same or a greater number of units.

    D. producers are trying to sell more units of a good or a service than consumers want to purchase at a particular price.

5. The Law of Demand says that

    A. a lower price will tend to lead a consumer to buy either the same or a greater amount of the good or service.

    B. consumers want to buy more units of something than producers want to sell at a particular price.

    C. as the market price of a good or service rises, producers offer the same or a greater number of units.

    D. producers are trying to sell more units of a good or a service than consumers want to purchase at a particular price.

6. Another word for a surplus is a

    A. glut

    B. shortage

    C. equilibrium

    D. premium

Short Answer:
On the lines provided, answer the questions in 1 to 3 sentences.

7. Define supply (not the Law of Supply).

_____

_____

_____

_____

_____

_____

_____

_____

_____

_____

8. Define demand (not the Law of Demand).

_____

_____

_____

_____

_____

_____

_____

_____

_____

_____

9. Why is it called an "equilibrium" price when quantity demanded equals quantity supplied?

_____

_____

_____

_____

_____

_____

_____

_____

10. Explain how the demand for something can remain constant, but the quantity demanded can decline.

_____

_____

_____

_____

_____

_____

_____

_____

_____

11. Explain how a glut in the orange market can be bad news for the producers of apples.

_____

_____

_____

_____

_____

_____

_____

_____

_____

_____

Multiple Choice:

1. B	2. C	3. D
4. C	5. A	6. A

Short Answer:

7. Define supply (not the Law of Supply).

SAMPLE FULL CREDIT ANSWER
The relationship between hypothetical prices and the quantity of a good or service that producers want to sell at each price.

SAMPLE PARTIAL CREDIT ANSWER
How much producers want to sell.

SAMPLE NO CREDIT ANSWER
Producers sell more at higher prices.

8. Define demand (not the Law of Demand).

SAMPLE FULL CREDIT ANSWER
The relationship between hypothetical prices and the quantity of a good or service that consumers want to buy at each price.

SAMPLE PARTIAL CREDIT ANSWER
How much consumers want to buy.

SAMPLE NO CREDIT ANSWER
Consumers buy more at lower prices.

9. Why is it called an "equilibrium" price when quantity demanded equals quantity supplied?

SAMPLE FULL CREDIT ANSWER
If the price were higher than the equilibrium price, there would be a surplus and producers would lower prices to move the unsold stock. If the price were lower than the equilibrium price, there would be a shortage and consumers would bid up the price on the available stock. Only at the equilibrium price is there no incentive for the price to move away, hence it is a stable position for the price.

SAMPLE PARTIAL CREDIT ANSWER
It is a stable point.

SAMPLE NO CREDIT ANSWER
It is the efficient point that makes everyone better off.

10. Explain how the demand for something can remain constant, but the quantity demanded can decline.

SAMPLE FULL CREDIT ANSWER
If the price goes up, then we move along the original demand curve. The curve itself stays put, so "demand" is constant, but at the higher price there is a lower quantity demanded.

SAMPLE PARTIAL CREDIT ANSWER
The price can change.

SAMPLE NO CREDIT ANSWER
Supply could also change.

11. Explain how a glut in the orange market can be bad news for the producers of apples.

SAMPLE FULL CREDIT ANSWER

A glut in the orange market will probably lead to lower orange prices. Then, since oranges are substitutes for apples (at least for many consumers), the lower orange prices will lead to a leftward shift in the demand for apples. Apple producers will therefore earn a lower price on apples.

SAMPLE PARTIAL CREDIT ANSWER

It will push down the price of apples.

SAMPLE NO CREDIT ANSWER

The apple producers might eat oranges too.

Interest, Credit, and Debt

Interest: It's About Time

As the student text indicates, the theory of interest is one of the most complicated areas in economics. Naturally we are not going to reproduce or even allude to the high-level debates among economists over the nature and causes of interest. Most economists would agree with the statements we make in this chapter, although some of them might have included other claims—such as the idea that the interest rate reflects the "productivity of capital"—that we are consciously omitting because they are actually controversial in certain camps.

The analogy between interest rates and currency exchange rates is meant to help the advanced student. If a student is struggling with the point, you can safely skip it. There is no point in burdening the student with an *extra* concept (exchange rates) just to shed light on the topic of interest.

It is important, however, that all students take away the idea that interest rates in a free market help to coordinate the actions of savers and investors. In particular, when the community saves more and frees up resources, (other things equal) interest rates fall and give the signal to entrepreneurs to invest resources in longer projects. The student will need to know this in order to make sense of the business cycle theory presented in Lesson 23.

Savings, Investment, and Economic Growth

The material in this section is fairly orthodox. The student who plans on taking an undergraduate course in economics, or who wants to view Roger Garrison's PowerPoint presentations (listed in the Supplemental Materials in Lesson 23), should understand how to use basic supply and demand analysis in the context of the loanable funds market.

The only real trick here is to understand the sense in which the interest rate is the "price" of a loan. If it helps, you can walk the student through and point out that we could just as well say the price of borrowing $1,000 for a year is $80 (payable at the time of repayment of the principal), in which case the interest rate is 8%. If the student is confused about the use of a percentage rather than an absolute dollar amount, you can explain that the special thing about interest is that people are renting the use of money. If a community used, say, tuxedos as money, then the rental price of a tux (for a junior prom) might be quoted in percentage terms too. But we use dollars as money, not tuxedos, and so the men's clothing store will quote a price in dollar terms for the temporary use of a tuxedo, which is why a percentage quote would make no sense. Yet in our world it *does* make sense for a *bank* to give a percentage quote on the price of a loan, since a loan is "renting money" and you pay for the service with money.

Common Credit Transactions

You will have to decide whether to stress the point that credit transactions per se do not increase the money supply. In order to think about difficult questions such as the likelihood of rising prices in the wake of the Fed's bailouts of the banking sector, it is crucial for the analyst to understand exactly how the money supply and credit interact with each other. (There is a further complication in our fractional reserve banking system, in which new bank loans *do* expand the quantity of money.) However, this might be too subtle a point for some students. For the truly advanced student who wants to learn the accounting treatment of modern fractional-reserve banking, consult this video lecture: **http://www.youtube.com/watch?v=6HAEPSt_12U.**

Bonds

The concept of bonds can be very intimidating, so you should make sure that the student understands it is simply a formalized way of borrowing money. When a corporation "sells" or "issues" a new bond, it is not producing something like a TV. It is simply borrowing money, in exchange for a standardized IOU spelling out the terms of the loan. The advantage of a bond issue (versus drawing up specific loan contracts with different lenders) is that it's very easy for the initial lender to sell the bond to someone else, and thus transfer the identity of the person to whom the corporation owes the remaining interest and principal payments.

Banks

Be sure the student understands the legitimate function that credit intermediaries serve, in assessing and spreading risk. Just as middlemen (and women) in physical products provide a definite service when they (say) buy oranges at a low price from Florida growers, and then sell them at a higher price in New York, by the same token the banks perform a valuable service when they borrow at a low rate and lend at a higher rate.

The student text did not spell it out, but all parties—including the lenders and the borrowers—benefit from the existence of banks, at least if we assume that the banks do their jobs properly and make sound loans. (This doesn't always occur, of course; the late 1920s and the late 2000s are great examples. However many economists would argue that this poor performance by the banks was caused or at least exacerbated by the government and Federal Reserve.)

Credit Cards

In the student text we have tried to be neutral, as many parents do not want their children ever using credit cards for obvious reasons. Economists must be able to explain the operations of this market, just as they need to understand how farmers and others fit into the cigarette market. Naturally the fact that some people buy cigarettes doesn't mean economists endorse smoking.

The Pros and Cons of Debt

Again, we have tried to be as evenhanded as possible in this section. Although few parents would glamorize high consumption financed through credit cards, most people do not have a principled objection to using mortgages to buy a starter house, or buying a car at least partially on credit. Pushing it even further, there would be far fewer doctors if no one were willing to take out loans to pay for medical school.

● ●

STUDY QUESTIONS

1. Why is the first section titled, "Interest: It's About Time"?

Interest rates coordinate the actions of savers and investors. When people postpone consumption today, it frees up resources that can begin producing the goods and services that the savers will buy in the future.

2. *What is the connection between interest rates and currency exchange rates?

Interest rates allow entrepreneurs to convert money units from different years into a common denominator. Currency exchange rates allow entrepreneurs to convert money units from different countries into a common denominator.

3. Why does a low interest rate give a "green light" to long production processes?

Entrepreneurs must buy inputs first, then sell the output later. The lower the interest rate, the more valuable the future revenue from customers will appear in today's calculations. Therefore, a given process with fixed dollar payments for inputs in the beginning, and a fixed dollar payment by customers at the end, will appear more profitable as the interest rate gets lower and lower.

4. What is exchanged in a credit transaction?

The lender gives money in exchange for an IOU from the borrower.

5. What is "productive debt"?

Debt that is used by the borrower in the hopes of increasing his or her future income.

Supplemental Materials

- Henry Hazlitt, *Economics In One Lesson*, Chapter VI.

  Hazlitt illustrates the harmful outcome when government uses credit to divert production. His analysis shows, however, that credit provided voluntarily by lenders on the free market leads to the beneficial results desired by the proponents of government loans to business.

- Thomas Woods, "Credit Diverts Production," interviewed by Jeff Tucker, audio at **http://mises.org/media/4300.**

  Woods provides commentary on the Hazlitt chapter.

- Murray Rothbard, *Man, Economy, and State*, pp. 367–89.

  This excerpt contains Rothbard's explanation for the determination of the pure interest rate on a market economy. It can be quite technical at times, and so only the most advanced students should even attempt it. But for those who have been following along with Rothbard, it should provide a complementary discussion to the much simpler presentation in the student text.

SUGGESTED ACTIVITIES

(1) For the truly advanced student, you could elaborate on the tuxedo analogy presented above. At first it might seem impossible for a young guy to rent a tuxedo on a Friday, and then return not only that same tuxedo, but the "interest" payment of another tuxedo (or a piece of one—maybe a vest) the following Monday. Yet note that this is exactly what happens when we borrow dollars from a bank—we are expected to return more dollar bills than the bank originally handed to us. Remind the student that by hypothesis, tuxedos are money. So the loan could be a productive loan in the literal sense, where (say) the borrower puts on the tuxedo and performs a lounge singer routine, in exchange for payment in the form of tuxedos. But it's also possible that the borrower uses the lent tuxedo to hire workers to make something which he then sells to customers for money (i.e., tuxedos), before paying off the loan plus interest. The point of this rather silly thought experiment is to drive home exactly what's happening with loans and interest, and why tuxedos would be an awfully inconvenient money.

(2) If appropriate, you could go over a credit report or the mortgage statement with the student, explaining the various items. Many newcomers are shocked when they first see how much of a mortgage or car payment goes toward interest in the early years; it may be worthwhile to explain this phenomenon. (In order to yield fixed monthly payments at a fixed interest rate, the earlier payments will necessarily involve more payment of interest and less reduction of principal, compared to later payments. The outstanding principal shrinks over time with further payments, and so [at a fixed interest rate] it grows less

after each payment knocks it down ever further. The process snowballs until the very last payment is devoted almost entirely to principal reduction, and completely pays off the loan.) You can google for "online amortization calculators" if students want to play with various numbers, to see for example the difference between buying a given house with a 15-year versus a 30-year mortgage at a given interest rate. (In the former case, the monthly payments are much higher, but the house is paid off in half the time and there are fewer "total dollars" going to interest payments over the life of the mortgage, which some people consider an important point although many economists would say such a statistic is somewhat misleading.)

(3) The student can experiment with the Federal Reserve's online database to look at various interest rates on different types of corporate bonds: **http://research. stlouisfed.org/fred2/categories/119**. You can explain that the safer bonds—which are given a better rating by the agencies—have a lower yield (interest rate), because investors are less worried that the borrowing corporation will default on the loan. Advanced students should recognize that there isn't "the" interest rate in a market economy, but actually a whole suite of interest rates based on the maturity time as well as the risk of the loan. The student can see points on the "yield curve"—the difference in interest rates even on debt issued by the same U.S. government, depending on the length of the loan—at this site: **http://research.stlouisfed.org/ fred2/categories/115**.

Multiple Choice:
Write the letter of the best answer.

1. This compensates lenders for giving up money available to them now, in exchange for a promise to be paid back with money not available until the future.

    A. principal
    B. credit
    C. debt
    D. interest

2. The _____ shows us exactly what the discount on future dollars is, or (equivalently) what the premium on current dollars is.

    A. exchange rate
    B. maturities rate
    C. market interest rate
    D. commodities market

3. An _____ rate is between currencies (e.g., U.S. Dollar vs. Japanese yen).

    A. interest
    B. exchange
    C. omninational
    D. international

4. Interest is not the "price of money." It is the "price of _____ money."

    A. borrowing

    B. earning

    C. saving

    D. lending

5. Secured loans are backed by

    A. the government

    B. collateral

    C. credit history

    D. credit intermediaries

6. Debt incurred by an entrepreneur for the purpose of expanding his or her business operations is called

    A. secured debt

    B. unsecured debt

    C. collateral debt

    D. productive debt

Short Answer:
On the lines provided, answer the questions in 1 to 3 sentences.

7. Justin forgot his lunch money at home. To make matters worse, it was pizza day at school, and Justin loves pizza. However, his friend, Vraj, always has money, so Justin asks if he can borrow $2.00. Vraj agrees, but insists upon being paid back $2.50 the next day. Calculate the (daily) interest rate of Vraj's loan.

_____

_____

_____

_____

_____

_____

_____

8. Explain why the deal between Justin and Vraj was mutually beneficial.

_____

_____

_____

_____

_____

_____

_____

_____

_____

9. Other things equal, an increase in interest rates will have what effect on the quantity demanded of loans?

_____

_____

_____

_____

_____

_____

_____

_____

10. Identify what happens to interest rates when a community saves more in general, and generalize the signal that this sends to entrepreneurs.

_____

_____

_____

_____

_____

_____

_____

_____

_____

_____

11. When a company sells a bond, what is it essentially doing?

_____

_____

_____

_____

_____

_____

_____

_____

_____

_____

12. What is the economic benefit of a credit intermediary such as a bank?

_____

_____

_____

_____

_____

_____

_____

_____

_____

_____

_____

13. Discuss this statement: "Getting rid of all records of credit histories and credit reports would help borrowers."

_____

_____

_____

_____

_____

_____

_____

_____

_____

14. Explain why the interest rates on unsecured loans tend to be higher than those on secured loans.

_____

_____

_____

_____

_____

_____

_____

_____

_____

_____

Multiple Choice:

1. D   2. C   3. B

4. A   5. B   6. D

Short Answer:

7. Justin forgot his lunch money at home. To make matters worse, it was pizza day at school, and Justin loves pizza. However, his friend, Vraj, always has money, so Justin asks if he can borrow $2.00. Vraj agrees, but insists upon being paid back $2.50 the next day. Calculate the (daily) interest rate of Vraj's loan.

25%.
[50 cents in interest divided by the original amount of $2 = 25%.]

8. Explain why the deal between Justin and Vraj was mutually beneficial.

SAMPLE FULL CREDIT ANSWER
Both agreed to it, so we know it was mutually beneficial. Justin got to eat his pizza, which he valued more than giving up the future 50 cents in interest, and Vraj earned the interest, which he valued more than what he otherwise could have done with his $2 the day he lent it.

SAMPLE PARTIAL CREDIT ANSWER
Both agreed to it.

SAMPLE NO CREDIT ANSWER
Someday the roles might be reversed. [NOTE: This is actually a true and relevant statement, but it clearly misses the whole point of the question/lesson.]

9. Other things equal, an increase in interest rates will have what effect on the quantity demanded of loans?

SAMPLE FULL CREDIT ANSWER
People will demand fewer loans or loans of a smaller amount.

10. Identify what happens to interest rates when a community saves more in general, and generalize the signal that this sends to entrepreneurs.

SAMPLE FULL CREDIT ANSWER
Interest rates tend to go down when people save more. This effectively signals entrepreneurs that they should borrow and invest
more, in longer-term projects.

SAMPLE PARTIAL CREDIT ANSWER
Interest rates go down.

SAMPLE NO CREDIT ANSWER
Businesses lay off workers because of lower spending.

11. When a company sells a bond, what is it essentially doing?

SAMPLE FULL CREDIT ANSWER
It is borrowing money.

12. What is the economic benefit of a credit intermediary such as a bank?

SAMPLE FULL CREDIT ANSWER
The bank matches up savers with borrowers. The bank's presence helps lower the cost of finding each other, and it makes the
process safer for lenders.

SAMPLE PARTIAL CREDIT ANSWER
Businesses that need funds can borrow them from a bank.

SAMPLE NO CREDIT ANSWER
Without banks, there would be no money to borrow.

13. Discuss this statement: "Getting rid of all records of credit histories and credit reports would help borrowers."

SAMPLE FULL CREDIT ANSWER
Without having access to a person's past behavior, a potential lender might assume the worst and charge a high interest rate. The responsible borrowers would end up being worse off, without the ability to demonstrate their good track record.

SAMPLE PARTIAL CREDIT ANSWER
This would be bad because lenders rely on that information.

SAMPLE NO CREDIT ANSWER
It would make borrowers better off but it would still be a bad thing to do.

14. Explain why the interest rates on unsecured loans tend to be higher than those on secured loans.

SAMPLE FULL CREDIT ANSWER
If the borrower defaults on a secured loan, the lender can repossess the collateral to offset the loss. If the borrower defaults on an unsecured loan, the lender has no recourse. To compensate for the added risk, a lender will charge more (other things equal) for an unsecured loan.

SAMPLE PARTIAL CREDIT ANSWER
They are riskier.

SAMPLE NO CREDIT ANSWER
Lenders can charge more to people without a lot of property.

Profit and Loss Accounting

Profit and Loss Guide Entrepreneurs

This section contains one of the most important insights in the entire course. Most people do not understand that the economy is a *dynamic* system in which people must always respond to changing conditions, be they unexpected weather, changes in consumer tastes, or a new invention. Make sure the student really understands how profits and losses guide entrepreneurs. There is no objective "right way" to run a business in a particular industry; entrepreneurs need to *discover* this through competition. (The Hayek reading in the Supplemental Materials elaborates on this important point, though it may be too difficult reading for some students.)

As a consequence, when we see businesses in the real world earning "excessive" profits, that isn't a signal that the owners are ripping people off. On the contrary, it's a signal that the owners are adjusting serious imbalances (or "false prices") in the market.

Interest versus Profit

You will have to determine how far to push this section, based on the ability of the student. The most basic point is that a company is not necessarily using resources efficiently just because it takes in more total dollars in sales than it pays out in expenses. Even if a business "turns a profit" in the every-day sense of the term, it might be suffering an *economic* loss once the implicit interest on the invested capital is taken into account.

For the more advanced student, there is a related point: It's actually not true (as we implied in Lesson 9) that competi-tion among entrepreneurs drives the "markup" to *zero*. This is because in a typical industry, there is a time delay (often siz-able) between the payment of wages and other expenses, ver-sus the receipt of the revenues from customers. Competition will still tend to bid up wages for workers, and push down prices for the final products, until the workers get paid the full value of their marginal contribution to the firm's revenues. However, the "full value" needs to take into account the time value of money. If a worker digs a ditch in the year 2010 for a shopping mall that won't be open to customers until the year 2012, then the entrepreneurs who pay the worker will take into account the fact that his wages are in 2010 dollars, which are worth more than 2012 dollars. So even if the worker ultimately contributes, say, $15 in revenues for every hour he spends dig-ging the ditch, he will only be paid (say) $13.61 per hour in 2010, if the interest rate is 5%. (Note that $13.61 x 1.05 x 1.05 = $15.)

This latter point is rather subtle, and you can safely skip it entirely for the beginning student. But more advanced stu-dents should recognize that competition doesn't actually whittle away "markups" to zero, in production processes that involve long periods of time. In a sense the markup really *does* get driven toward zero, once we convert dollars from differ-ent time periods into a common denominator; but still this is a subtle point that many people never think about, and you should clarify it for the advanced student.

The Social Function of Profit and Loss Accounting

The Austrians are rare among economists because they can really explain the social function of profit and loss accounting. Mainstream economists focus on equilibrium states in which there are no profit opportunities; they take up the analysis at the point where competition has already *eliminated* any price discrepancies. For the Austrian, this is to ignore the heart of the market economy, when entrepreneurs make adjustments in an attempt to better satisfy the consumers.

The material in this section follows the presentation by Robert Murphy (listed below in the Supplemental Materials). However, that discussion can become somewhat technical in the second half.

The Limits of Profit and Loss Accounting

Be sure that the student doesn't draw the wrong conclusion from this chapter. We are not saying that entrepreneurs need to do whatever makes the most profit. All we are saying is that the profit and loss system provides a mental aid to entrepreneurs as they run their businesses, buying resources from one group of people, turning them into products and services, and then selling the output to other people. Without market prices for each component in this complicated process, the entrepreneurs would be "groping in the dark," as Mises says. It's crucial for students to understand this point now, in order to make sense of the chapters on socialism later on.

But just because something is necessary for guidance, doesn't mean that it should be the master. For an analogy, if a family goes to Disneyland for the first time, they will surely want to obtain a map of the park. The map doesn't force the family to visit rides in a particular sequence, but it provides crucial information for the family to make its decisions. Without the map, they would be "groping in the dark," stumbling from one ride to the next and having no idea if they were spending their hours (and leg muscles) in the best way, given their own desires and the physical layout of the park.

• •

STUDY QUESTIONS

1. Explain: "Entrepreneurs do not respond to particular prices but rather to the difference between certain prices."

Most entrepreneurs are not out to maximize revenues, but rather to earn profits. Monetary profit is the difference between the revenues from customers and the expenditures on inputs. Just because a particular price is very high doesn't automatically mean that entrepreneurs rush to produce the item in question; the expenses involved in producing the item might be really high too.

2. Explain: "In a market economy with open competition, there is a tendency for monetary profits and losses to be whittled away over time, as entrepreneurs adjust to the situation."

If the prices in a certain industry allow the firms to reap large monetary profits, this will tend to attract competitors. By producing more of the finished good (or service), they push down its price, and by buying more of the inputs needed to produce it, they push up the costs of production. Thus the overall profit margin shrinks. The reverse happens in an industry suffering from monetary losses.

3. *How does interest relate to profit, specifically the difference between accounting and economic profit?

In everyday language, and even in terms of standard accounting, "profit" refers to the excess of money receipts over money expenditures. But this figure includes the interest payment on the invested capital in the business. In other words, out of the gross or accounting profit we need to subtract the interest payment reflecting the fact that the investors' capital was tied up for a certain period when it could have been "at work" in another project.

Explain?

4. In what sense do consumers—rather than the "captains of industry"—guide the production decisions in a market economy?

With their spending decisions, consumers provide guidance to entrepreneurs, to the extent that they allow themselves to be steered by considerations of (monetary) profit. It is the spending of smokers that leads farmers to plant tobacco.

5. Does a market economy force entrepreneurs to do whatever makes the most profit?

No, in a market economy the owner determines the fate of a particular unit of resources (including labor services). No matter how high the price of cigarettes, a farmer doesn't have to plant tobacco if he doesn't want to. But market prices do allow resource owners to make informed decisions. They get a sense of how much other people want to encourage them to use their resources in a particular way.

Supplemental Materials

- Ludwig von Mises, "Profit and Loss," Sections 1–5, at **http:// mises.org/story/2321**.

   Although Mises's writings are always formal, this is actually an accessible introduction to Mises's views on profit and loss. His analysis covers much of the same ground as our (simplified) student lesson.

- Joe Salerno, "The Theory of Profit, Loss, and Entrepreneurship," audio at **http://mises.org/media/1027**.

   Salerno provides an introduction to the Austrian understanding. Although other schools of economic thought give a cursory nod to the role of the entrepreneur, the Austrians emphasize entrepreneurship probably more than any other school. This relates to the relatively narrow importance Austrians ascribe to the analysis of equilibrium states, focusing instead on the process by which an economy moves toward equilibrium.

- Robert Murphy, "Consumer Sovereignty and the Production Process," audio at **http://mises.org/media/4004**.

   In this lecture Murphy first explains Mises's endorsement of the notion of "consumer sovereignty" and why a market economy usually satisfies this principle. Then Murphy explains the Rothbardian critique of the concept. Part of the discussion involves monopoly theory, which the student can safely omit. (Murphy has also written articles on these topics, available at **http://mises.org/daily/1364 and http:// mises.org/daily/1379**.)

- Friedrich Hayek, "Competition as a Discovery Procedure," at **https://mises.org/journals/qjae/pdf/qjae5_3_3.pdf**.

   This is a classic Hayek paper but it is formal. Even if they can't understand all of it, most students should probably be encouraged to at least try reading it.

SUGGESTED ACTIVITIES

Look through a newspaper or online financial website to see discussions of earnings or "profits" of major corporations. Explain that these are accounting profits. Investors who leave their money tied up in a corporation must look at their return (whether measured in dividend payments or increase in the stock price) and compare it with other places they could have invested their money during the same time period. It's not enough to know, for example, that the Acme Corporation took in $1 billion in revenues and paid out $990 million in expenses. That $10 million in profits could be wonderful if Acme is a lemonade stand company with just the labor of the thirteen-year-old owner being the non-compensated input. (The $990 million paid for an enormous amount of lemonade mix, disposable cups, etc.) On the other hand, if Acme runs an offshore oil rig that took $5 billion of investments to construct, then having a particular year—once it's in full operation—where revenues were only $10 million higher than out-of-pocket expenses is probably disastrous, compared to other, safer investment opportunities. (This is because the investors would only be earning a 2% return on their $5 billion investment, when they probably could have earned a higher rate of return by investing in bonds or other lines that were safer than an offshore oil rig. We aren't even considering the fact that the oil rig would take a long time to construct, a period during which the rate of return on investment would be zero.)

Short Answer:
On the lines provided, answer the questions in 1 to 3 sentences.

1. Explain why, generally speaking, activities that generate high (monetary) profits will attract more entrepreneurs, while those that cause losses will repel entrepreneurs.

_____

_____

_____

_____

_____

_____

_____

_____

2. Explain the distinction economists often make between interest and profit.

_____

_____

_____

_____

_____

_____

_____

_____

_____

_____

3. Does the profit and loss system force movie theaters to stay open on Christmas? Explain.

_____

_____

_____

_____

_____

_____

_____

_____

_____

4. Explain how the profit and loss system communicates the desires of consumers to resource owners and entrepreneurs.

_____

_____

_____

_____

_____

_____

_____

_____

_____

_____

_____

5. If smoking is bad for you, then why do farmers grow tobacco?

_____

_____

_____

_____

_____

_____

_____

_____

_____

_____

Short Answer:

1. Explain why, generally speaking, activities that generate high (monetary) profits will attract more entrepreneurs, while those that cause losses will repel entrepreneurs.

SAMPLE FULL CREDIT ANSWER
Although there are other motivations, generally speaking people go into business to earn monetary profits. In general, entrepreneurs will mimic those activities that are generating monetary profits for other people, and they will stop doing those activities that are causing losses. By acting in this fashion, entrepreneurs try to earn as much monetary profit as they can, other things equal.

SAMPLE PARTIAL CREDIT ANSWER
If a business keeps losing money, eventually it will go bankrupt.

SAMPLE NO CREDIT ANSWER
People only care about money in a capitalist system.

2. Explain the distinction economists often make between interest and profit.

SAMPLE FULL CREDIT ANSWER
Gross or accounting profit is total revenue minus out-of-pocket expenditures. However, this calculation ignores the interest on the invested capital. Even if a business venture "makes money," if the investor could have ended up with even more money through a different (and equally safe) investment, then in a sense the investor actually suffered a loss.

SAMPLE PARTIAL CREDIT ANSWER
Profit can mislead if it doesn't include interest.

SAMPLE NO CREDIT ANSWER
If an investor puts his money in a business, he earns profits, but if he puts it in bonds, he earns interest.

3. Does the profit and loss system force movie theaters to stay open on Christmas? Explain.

SAMPLE FULL CREDIT ANSWER
No, the owners of theaters always have the ability to keep them closed on holidays. Yet very few owners exercise this right, because it is so profitable to have movies open on holidays. The profit and loss system communicates to the owners how much people want to watch movies on their holiday breaks.

SAMPLE PARTIAL CREDIT ANSWER
No, they can close down if they want to.

SAMPLE NO CREDIT ANSWER
Yes but it's good for people who watch movies.

4. Explain how the profit and loss system communicates the desires of consumers to resource owners and entrepreneurs.

SAMPLE FULL CREDIT ANSWER
Through their spending decisions, consumers give entrepreneurs the money with which they bid on worker hours, oil, land, equip- ment, and other inputs. The prices of the inputs reflect how urgently those resources are needed in certain lines, to produce particular goods and services that some consumers desire. Loosely speaking, a profitable business is taking undervalued resources and transforming them into outputs that have a higher value, while an unprofitable business is wasting resources on projects that are not as valuable as alternatives.

SAMPLE PARTIAL CREDIT ANSWER
If consumers want something they will pay a lot for it.

SAMPLE NO CREDIT ANSWER
Entrepreneurs want to make money.

5. If smoking is bad for you, then why do farmers grow tobacco?

SAMPLE FULL CREDIT ANSWER

Some consumers are smokers and are willing to pay a lot of money for cigarettes. Companies then find it worthwhile to spend a lot on tobacco in order to produce cigarettes. The high price of tobacco makes it attractive for some farmers to plant it, rather than other crops.

SAMPLE PARTIAL CREDIT ANSWER

To make money.

SAMPLE NO CREDIT ANSWER

People can be addicted even if they want to stop smoking.

The Stock Market

The Stock Market

There is an entire field of financial economics that studies issues such as the pricing of corporate stock, the relative merits of issuing debt versus equity, and so on. In this introductory course we are obviously not going to cover such controversies and rival theories. Rather, we are trying to give the student a basic understanding of what the stock market is and how the principles of previous chapters apply in this setting.

If you take a course in financial economics at a highly ranked university, it will be extremely quantitative, more so than most other areas of economic theory; in this respect typical financial economists are very different from the typical Austrian economist. However, many of the practitioners in this field are very sympathetic to free-market principles and recognize the harm of government intervention in financial markets. For whatever reason, there is a large body of academics who recognize the benefits of unfettered entrepreneurship in the narrow realm of stocks and bonds, whereas these same academics might be more skeptical of laissez-faire in the market for teenage labor and electricity.

Why Issue Stock? (Debt versus Equity)

The ostensible purpose of this section is to compare two different methods of raising funds, namely issuing debt versus equity. However, this particular question isn't very important for our purposes. Rather, we are going through this discussion because it offers a concrete, real-world problem that gives us an opportunity to introduce new concepts that are relevant to this chapter.

In other words, the student shouldn't get bogged down trying to memorize the pros and cons of debt versus equity. Rather, the student should grasp the essence of what debt and equity *are*, and we hope that framing the issue in terms of a corporation trying to raise money will be interesting to the student.

The Social Function of Stock Speculation

One of the most hated figures in the world is the speculator, in particular a financial speculator. To some people, someone who makes money by, say, betting against a Latin American currency is the lowest form of evil. Whenever speculators "attack" the currency of a profligate government that has run up an excessive debt and has printed too much money, the government officials naturally claim that the speculators are the *cause* of the weak currency.

As this section demonstrates, successful speculators actually *reduce* the volatility of an asset, in the following sense: If a speculator buys low and sells high, then his very actions tend to push up the price when it was initially low, and push down the price when it becomes high. Thus the speculator reduces the gap in prices that otherwise would have existed.

Depending on the student, you may want to elaborate and explain that this explanation is a bit too simplistic. In the real world, we can imagine speculators initially being successful by starting an "asset bubble." For example, if speculators begin a mass buying spree of houses, this may set into motion a self-fulfilling prophecy where further speculative buying pushes up the price still further, and apparently justifies the initial round of buying. However, if the "fundamentals" do not support this higher price, then eventually the bubble pops and the last speculators holding the bag suffer huge losses. In such a scenario, one could argue that the initial speculators—even though they made money—were harmful to society by pushing prices above their "correct" level. This is a deep issue and not all economists—not even all Austrian economists—agree on how to frame the matter. (The last reading in the Supplemental Materials elaborates on these matters.)

• •

STUDY QUESTIONS

1. If Jim owns 200 shares of a corporation, can we figure out how much of the corporation Jim owns?

No, we need to know the total number of shares as well, in order to calculate Jim's percentage. The point of this question is to make sure the student realizes corporations have different amounts of stock shares.

2. What are the two basic options a corporation can take to raise new funds?

The corporation can issue debt (i.e., sell bonds) or equity (i.e., sell new shares of stock).

3. Who gets first dibs on the earnings of a corporation—the bondholders or the stockholders?

The bondholders. The stockholders are residual claimants, meaning they are only entitled to the assets of the corporation after everyone else (suppliers, lenders, laid-off employees filing a lawsuit, customers demanding a refund, etc.) has been satisfied.

4. If a corporation is highly leveraged, will its stock be more likely to appeal to a conservative or an aggressive investor?

The "correct" answer is the aggressive investor. In reality even a conservative investor might own a small portion of a highly leveraged company, so long as the investor diversifies his holdings across many corporations. But in this basic question we are just trying to get the student to understand that—other things equal—more leverage tends to magnify potential gains and potential losses.

5. *How do successful speculators reduce the volatility of stock prices?

A stock price is volatile when it bounces around a lot, rather than moving within a narrow band. Stock speculators, if they are profitable, tend to reduce the band in which a stock price moves. If a stock price is above where it "should" be, the astute speculator will sell it, pushing down the price. If the price is originally too low, the astute speculator will buy the stock, pushing up the price.

Supplemental Materials

- Robert Murphy, "The Social Function of Stock Speculators," at **http://mises.org/daily/2381**.

   This is a slightly more formal exposition of the material in the student text.

- Robert Murphy, "A Man, A Plan, and a Short-Selling Ban," at **http://www.econlib.org/library/Columns/y2008/Murphyshortsell.html**.

   In the midst of the financial crisis, the SEC under the Bush administration made it temporarily illegal to "short sell" stock in certain vulnerable companies. This article explains the harm of such a policy.

- Robert Murphy, "Bursting Eugene Fama's Bubble," at **http://mises.org/daily/4056**.

   This article is only intended for advanced students. It criticizes famous Chicago economist Eugene Fama's use of the "efficient markets hypothesis" in light of the crash in housing prices around 2007. The material in the student textbook should not be taken to endorse all speculative activity, as the article on Fama makes clear. We are not claiming that speculators are always right, we are merely claiming that there are incentives for speculators to correctly anticipate price changes, and that successful speculation does indeed help others.

SUGGESTED ACTIVITIES

(1) One popular exercise is to have students assemble a "fantasy stock portfolio" (analogous to "fantasy football teams," etc.). Especially if you have multiple students, you can allocate each student an initial sum of money and have him or her spend it on blocks of stock from various corporations. You can then use a simple Excel file to track the movements of the total market value of each student's stock portfolio by plugging in the prices from a site such as **http://www.cnbc.com/**. (The student can enter the stock ticker in the search engine at the top of the main page.)

(2) You can have the student read financial articles either online or in a print newspaper such as the *Wall Street Journal*. The goal is not to have the student grapple with the opinions that are offered, but just to understand the basic terms used in a typical financial news story. For example, a stock price can go up even when the corporation reports losing money, just so long as "the market" had been expecting an even worse report. Fair warning: Much of the mainstream financial press is economically illiterate, as judged by the economic principles in this course. The student is not looking to the press to learn economics by any stretch. But a complete novice can start learning about the business world by occasionally watching CNBC or reading the *Wall Street Journal*.

(3) You can work through a simple numerical example to illustrate the effect of leverage. For example, suppose the managers of a corporation spot an opportunity to buy trinkets from an archeological dig in Peru at $10 and sell them to collectors in the U.S. a month later at $15.

Unfortunately the company only has $10,000 in cash that it can devote to this project. If the company spends all of its cash on this project, it will earn $5,000 total—a 50% return on its investment of $10,000—if the trinkets really can be sold for $15 apiece to collectors in the United States. On the other hand, if the trinkets turn out to be worthless, the corporation could lose up to $10,000 on the deal—a complete loss of 100%.

Now suppose the managers are extremely confident in the success of the project. They issue $10,000 worth of new corporate bonds, which mature in one month at which time the corporation will have to pay back the lenders a total of $10,100. Armed with these extra funds, the corporation initially buys 2,000 trinkets from the archeological dig site at $10 apiece. If they can turn around and unload them (as they expect) for $15 each in the U.S., then their total revenues will be $30,000. Out of that, they must pay $10,100 to the bondholders, leaving them with $19,900. Since they started out with $10,000 of their own money, their total monetary profit is $9,900, a return of 99%. (Compare that to the 50% return in the original scenario.) This is the advantage of leverage: when things go well, it magnifies the positive return.

On the other hand, suppose the trinkets cannot be sold for any money. In this case, the corporation is out not only its original $10,000, but also still owes the bondholders $10,100. In this case the total loss on the project would be $20,100, based on an original investment of the corporation's money of $10,000. That works out to a loss of 201%! With no leverage, the worst the corporation can do is lose everything on a deal, i.e., a loss of 100%. But with leverage—i.e., speculating with other people's money—the corporation can lose even more than that.

In the real world, corporations very rarely buy an asset only to see its price literally plummet to $0. However, in the real world many corporations are highly leveraged, sometimes as much as 30-to-1, meaning that they have borrowed $30 for every $1 in owners' assets involved in the corporation's operations. In such a position, even a slight reduction in the market value of the corporation's assets can spell bankruptcy.

(4) For a sufficiently advanced student, you could apply the discussion of debt versus equity to the problem of the financial crisis which began in the late 2000s. Many commentators have derided the low-interest policies of the Federal Reserve, saying, "The banks have plenty of liquidity. Their problem is that they are undercapitalized; they need the government to buy shares of stock, not make cheap loans." For students who have a basic understanding of accounting, our discussion of debt versus equity will shed light on this controversy over how to jump-start ailing banks. (Of course, we are neglecting the negative consequences of government intervention in the banking sector—our point here is to note the relevance of our abstract discussion in the student text to real-world controversies.)

Matching Essential Terminology:
Write the appropriate term on the line beside its description.

Stock exchange
Stock brokerage
Bonds
Dividend
Leverage
Speculator

1. _____ The size of a company's debt relative to the equity held by the owners.

2. _____ Where purchases and sales of (some) stock shares occur.

3. _____ A sum of money (from revenues) paid to shareholders.

4. _____ Someone who buys a particular stock because he looks to sell it at a profit in the near future.

5. _____ Companies that buy and sell stocks for people.

6. _____ What companies can sell to raise money, if they do not want to share ownership with others.

Short Answer:
On the lines provided, answer the questions in 1 to 3 sentences.

7. Explain why companies might want to raise outside funds, rather than financing any desired spending out of profits.

_____

_____

_____

_____

_____

_____

_____

_____

_____

8. Discuss the distinction between a corporation raising new funds by issuing debt versus stock.

_____

_____

_____

_____

_____

_____

_____

_____

_____

_____

9. Explain how speculators actually regulate the stock market in a healthy and non-interventionist way.

_____

_____

_____

_____

_____

_____

_____

_____

_____

10. In common discussions, what is the difference between an investor and a speculator in stocks?

_____

_____

_____

_____

_____

_____

_____

_____

_____

_____

Matching Essential Terminology:

1. Leverage   2. Stock exchange   3. Dividend

4. Speculator   5. Stock brokerage   6. Bonds

Short Answer:

7. Explain why companies might want to raise outside funds, rather than financing any desired spending out of profits.

SAMPLE FULL CREDIT ANSWER
A company might see an opportunity that it needs to seize quickly. For example, if a company thinks it can double its profits by building another $10 million factory, but only has $1 million in net income each year, it may want to raise the needed money from outsiders rather than wait (at least) ten years before expanding.

SAMPLE PARTIAL CREDIT ANSWER
A company thinks it can make more money.

SAMPLE NO CREDIT ANSWER
Borrowing money is risky.

8. Discuss the distinction between a corporation raising new funds by issuing debt versus stock.

SAMPLE FULL CREDIT ANSWER
When a corporation issues debt, its leverage increases and it is more vulnerable if its assets lose value. The upside is that if the corporation does well, it only owes the bondholders a fixed amount of interest payments. When a corporation issues stock, outsiders now share in the profits or losses, which cushions the blow but also reduces the potential gains to the original owners.

249

SAMPLE PARTIAL CREDIT ANSWER
Issuing debt is riskier.

SAMPLE NO CREDIT ANSWER
A corporation borrows money when it wants to expand.

9. Explain how speculators actually regulate the stock market in a healthy and non-interventionist way.

SAMPLE FULL CREDIT ANSWER
A speculator buys low and sells high, or short-sells high and buys back low. A successful speculator therefore bids up underpriced stocks, and pushes down overpriced stocks. Successful speculation therefore makes stock prices less volatile for other, less knowledgeable investors.

SAMPLE PARTIAL CREDIT ANSWER
Speculators correct mispricings in the stock market.

SAMPLE NO CREDIT ANSWER
Every sale in the stock market is voluntary, so speculators have no effect on regular investors.

10. In common discussions, what is the difference between an investor and a speculator in stocks?

SAMPLE FULL CREDIT ANSWER
People typically think of an investor as someone who intends to hold a stock for a long time either as part of a general strategy or because the company seems dependable. A speculator, on the other hand, is someone who looks to get in and out relatively quickly, after an anticipated price move.

SAMPLE PARTIAL CREDIT ANSWER
A speculator thinks the original price of the stock is wrong.

SAMPLE NO CREDIT ANSWER
A speculator wants to become richer.

Part III

SOCIALISM:
THE COMMAND
ECONOMY

The Failures of Socialism—Theory

The Vision of Pure Socialism

One of the greatest accomplishments of the Austrian School of economics was the critique of socialism developed by Ludwig von Mises in 1920, and elaborated by his follower Friedrich Hayek. (For a brief summary of the "socialist calculation debate" see the beginning of Robert Murphy's article available at **http://mises.org/journals/qjae/pdf/qjae9_2_1.pdf**.) Although every free market economist is familiar with the incentive problem of socialism, not all of them are aware of the calculation problem. We handle these different problems in the sections below.

We are assuming that the "vision of pure socialism" involves the government taking ownership of all factors of production. As we note in a footnote in the student text, some self-described socialists would *not* endorse this strategy. They reject government control of resources, but they do not endorse private property either. To such theorists, the system of capitalism itself represents an unjust concentration of power into the hands of an elite group. If the student is interested and wants to read more on the cutting-edge theoretical arguments from people who reject private property, a good starting point is this website: **http://www.infoshop.org/page/AnAnarchistFAQ.** (Note that for these writers, "anarchism" is not compatible with "capitalism.")

Socialism's Incentive Problem

To be clear on the outline of our presentation: In Part II of the student text, we described the operation of a pure market economy. In Part III we (more briefly) explain the problems with a pure command economy. In Part IV we will explain the undesirable consequences of limited government interventions into a market economy—i.e., we will describe what happens in a so-called mixed economy.

Breaking down the outline even further: In the present chapter (Lesson 15), we are discussing the *theoretical* problems with socialism. In the next chapter (Lesson 16), we will look at the *actual historical experience* of socialist governments.

And to break down the outline one more step: In the present chapter, we divide the theoretical critique of socialism into two components. First, in this section we discuss the incentive problem, which shows that total output will likely fall with the move to socialism, and also that the composition of output will likely be worse from the consumers' point of view. Then, in the next section we discuss the calculation problem, which is completely distinct from the incentive problem. In other words, even if the socialist reformers were correct, and people born in a socialist community were not selfish or abusive (so we didn't have to worry about the incentive problem), the central planners would still face the calculation problem.

Who Picks Up the Garbage?

This subsection makes two main points. First, once we depart from the market economy's principle of paying a worker in proportion to his or her marginal product, we encounter the problem of getting people to do "dirty work." If it weren't for differences of pay, most people would prefer to pick up golf balls (at a driving range) rather than pick up trash cans (on a garbage truck route). Yes, there are other changes the socialist planners could make, in order to get more volunteers for a particular job, but then these changes would impact the output in other sectors. (One of the Suggested Activities relates to this issue.)

The second main point of this subsection is that even if the socialist planners were willing to use punishments to get the required number of "volunteers" in each occupation, they still wouldn't be able to mimic the outcome of a market economy. This is because you can't tell from simple inspection which workers are capable of genius. By definition, no one knows what amazing invention or discovery a person is capable of, until he or she invents or discovers it. So although the planners wouldn't need to worry about getting people to pick up the garbage—if they were willing to threaten workers who refused to do the dirty work—they still wouldn't be able to motivate everyone to perform the same as they would under a system of private property.

For the advanced student, you should make clear that the argument isn't simply that a potential genius needs the possibility of earning millions before he or she is willing to tinker in the laboratory. That observation is probably true for a large number of the practical inventions and discoveries made every year in a market economy, but it isn't necessary for our point. There are some tasks that slaves simply cannot do, and in a very real sense, the workers in a system of State-run socialism are all property of the government. To give a vivid example, suppose the planners unwittingly take the next Einstein or Edison and assign him to garbage truck duty! The physical labor and loud noises (if in a big city) might prevent would-be geniuses from ever contributing beyond their assigned tasks.

Allocating "Capital" to New "Firms"

All students should grasp the standard incentive problem discussed in the prior subsection. In this subsection, we explore a subtler but perhaps far more significant problem. It is hard enough to explain how a socialist system could match the performance of a market economy if things stayed the same, but once we realize that conditions constantly change, then the case for a market economy is even stronger. If the student understood the earlier discussion of the role of entrepreneurship and the stock market, then he or she should understand the immense disadvantages confronting a socialist system.

One Giant Monopoly

The "incentive problem" of socialism is typically used to denote the problem of workers who shirk when their pay is not directly tied to performance. However, in this subsection we spell out the problems on the other end, where the people in charge have little incentive to ensure customer satisfaction. (There is a Suggested Activity related to this subsection.)

Socialism's Calculation Problem

In this section we are scratching the surface of the "calculation argument" developed by Ludwig von Mises and Friedrich Hayek. This is one of the seminal contributions of the Austrian School and students who wish to learn more should follow up with the Supplemental Material.

The advanced student might notice that there is a partial overlap between the problem of allocating capital as discussed above (as part of the "incentive problem") and the more general calculation problem. The way to distinguish the two is the following: There is definitely an incentive problem when it comes to the central planners deciding upon various projects to fund, because they aren't experts in each field and so can't be sure if some of the promoters are lying or exaggerating in order to get resources for their own ideas. But even if we assume all of this away, and pretend that none of the promoters would do anything except render his or her honest judgment on all of the technical issues, nonetheless the central planners still wouldn't be able to calculate the *economically efficient* projects that deserved funding.

Solving the Calculation Problem?

In this subsection we repeat the rhetorical device used earlier, and show that in order to solve the problems of socialism, the central planners are led step by step back toward a market economy. This isn't attacking a strawman, incidentally: If you read the historical overview of the socialist calculation debate in the Murphy article in the Supplemental Materials, you will see that the socialist theorists introduced various forms of "market socialism" to deal with Mises's critique.

• •

STUDY QUESTIONS

1. Explain the term *command economy*.

The term refers to the fact that under (State) socialism, a group of a few (or one) political authorities controls all productive resources, including labor.

2. What is the incentive problem inherent in the slogan, "From each according to his ability, to each according to his needs"?

The policy of this slogan severs the connection between work and reward. It is unlikely that workers would contribute as much to the pile of total output, if the amount they got to consume (or give to their family) had nothing to do with their contribution.

3. Could a socialist government use punishment to overcome the problem of shirking among workers?

For certain, simple tasks—such as garbage collection and painting barns—a socialist government could use punishment to get workers to carry out their assigned duties. But many jobs require creativity and other unobservable aptitudes. A market economy allows workers to choose their own occupations and discover the fields where they can contribute the most. Even with the use of punishment, socialist officials wouldn't be able to force their subjects to produce the same output. (Could you really use a whip to force someone with nimble hands to spend years training to become a brain surgeon?)

4. What do beer companies and electric utilities have to do with socialism?

The argument in the text is that during summer months, companies that enjoy government-granted monopolies such as electric and water utilities often restrict their service, whereas private companies in open competition (such as beer and soda producers) welcome the boost in demand for their products.

5. *Why doesn't a market economy suffer from the same calculation problem that plagues the socialist planners?

The market overcomes the calculation problem because no one group is "in charge" who needs to decide everything. The decisions are instead dispersed among all the owners of producer goods (including labor). The profit and loss test, as revealed by market prices, guides the owners when they decide how to deploy their resources.

Supplemental Materials

- Gene Callahan, *Economics For Real People*, Chapter 10.

  Callahan covers much of the same territory in his
  chapter, as we have done in the student text (though
  in a different order). One thing to note is that the
  "knowledge problem" is very similar to the "calculation
  problem"; they both flow out of the writings of Mises
  and Hayek in their debate against the socialist theorists.
  (Specifically, the knowledge problem refers to the
  inability of central planners to actually assemble all
  the information they would need in order to rationally
  design the economy, whereas the calculation problem
  in its purest form takes this information as given and
  still says that the planners would not know how best to
  deploy resources.) The knowledge/calculation problems
  are completely distinct from the incentive problem of
  socialism.

- Joe Salerno, "Calculation and Socialism," video at **http://mises.
  org/media/4366**.

  Salerno provides a good introduction to the calculation
  problem. His presentation doesn't assume too much
  on the part of the viewer, but the presentation is more
  formal than Callahan's discussion.

- Mateusz Machaj, "The Nature of Socialism," at **http://mises.
  org/daily/4066**.

  Machaj's article is the most formal of the three selections,
  and beginner students should probably skip it. The
  article is part of a collection in honor of Hans Hoppe,
  and thus it is geared toward an academic audience.
  Even so, it is easier reading than the actual articles
  in the historical calculation debate, and provides an
  intermediate stepping stone for the advanced student
  who may wish to jump in.

SUGGESTED ACTIVITIES

(1) Have the student identify appealing versus distasteful jobs that require comparable skill levels. (For example, serving food in Disneyworld versus serving food to the workers at a chicken slaughterhouse.) If the central planners are not allowed to pay more for the distasteful occupations, what other incentives could they use to prevent everyone from volunteering for the appealing jobs and no volunteering for the distasteful ones? (For example, the planners could insist that everyone who volunteers to work at Disneyworld first pass a difficult trigonometry exam, or that anyone who volunteers at the slaughterhouse gets to have lunch with a movie star once per year.) Have the student think through the implications of these changes.

(2) Have the student keep track of differences in the attention to customer satisfaction when it comes to private businesses versus government agencies or private agencies that enjoy a government-granted monopoly. (This last category includes the Post Office and many local utilities.) The differences could include items such as ease of finding a parking spot, hours of operation (e.g., check out the hours of your local "public" library and compare them to hours of a book store or video rental business), time spent waiting in line, and friendliness of staff.

Multiple Choice:
Write the letter of the best answer to each question.

1. In a command economy, resources are owned and controlled by
    A. capitalists.
    B. the people.
    C. the government.
    D. producers.

2. Capitalism is to market economy as _____ is to command economy.
    A. anarchism
    B. socialism
    C. egalitarianism
    D. monarchism
    E. Obamism

3. Which economist systematically laid out the calculation objection to socialism?
    A. Karl Marx
    B. Adam Smith
    C. David Hume
    D. Ludwig von Mises

263

Short Answer:
On the lines provided, answer the questions in 1 to 3 sentences.

4. What is the incentive problem for workers under socialism?

_____

_____

_____

_____

_____

_____

_____

_____

5. Describe socialism's "calculation problem" (which is NOT the same as the incentive problem).

_____

_____

_____

_____

_____

_____

_____

_____

_____

6. What is ironic about the various schemes that can be implemented to "cure" socialism of its problems?

_____

_____

_____

_____

_____

_____

_____

_____

_____

_____

7. Explain why you probably receive better service at Walmart than at the Department of Motor Vehicles.

_____

_____

_____

_____

_____

_____

_____

_____

_____

_____

_____

_____

8. Contrast the very worst that a capitalist "tyrant" can do to you (as a malcontented worker or an obnoxious customer) versus what a socialist tyrant can do to you.

_____

_____

_____

_____

_____

_____

_____

_____

_____

_____

_____

_____

_____

_____

_____

_____

_____

_____

_____

_____

_____

_____

Multiple Choice:

1. C　　　　2. B　　　　3. D

Short Answer:

4. What is the incentive problem for workers under socialism?

SAMPLE FULL CREDIT ANSWER
If people are not paid in accordance with their productive output—if they're paid according to "need"—then they might not work as hard under socialism as they would under capitalism. There would be fewer goods and services produced overall, meaning that the average standard of living would have to fall.

SAMPLE PARTIAL CREDIT ANSWER
People would have no reason to work as hard.

SAMPLE NO CREDIT ANSWER
The rulers might turn out to be evil.

5. Describe socialism's "calculation problem" (which is NOT the same as the incentive problem).

SAMPLE FULL CREDIT ANSWER
If the government owns all of the resources, then there can be no market prices for them. That means the government, when drawing up the detailed plans for what should be produced, won't have any way to quantify the costs of their decisions. The planners won't know if they are using resources efficiently.

SAMPLE PARTIAL CREDIT ANSWER
The government won't be able to calculate if it is doing a good job in its plan for the economy.

SAMPLE NO CREDIT ANSWER
Workers might not work as hard.

6. What is ironic about the various schemes that can be implemented to "cure" socialism of its problems?

SAMPLE FULL CREDIT ANSWER
In order to solve the problems of socialism, the central planners might (say) allow workers to swap their finished goods with each other and to vote on what gets produced, and the planners might also allow the factory managers some discretion in how much they produce, based on their expectations of customer demand. Yet with each refinement, the system would more closely resemble capitalism.

SAMPLE PARTIAL CREDIT ANSWER
The socialist system turns into a capitalist one.

SAMPLE NO CREDIT ANSWER
No system can ever escape the imperfections of man.

7. Explain why you probably receive better service at Walmart than at the Department of Motor Vehicles.

SAMPLE FULL CREDIT ANSWER
The DMV has a monopoly on its "services" and thus has little incentive to keep its "customers" satisfied. In contrast, if Walmart employees consistently treat customers rudely, Walmart will lose market share and eventually go out of business if the problem is severe enough.

SAMPLE PARTIAL CREDIT ANSWER
Walmart has competition.

SAMPLE NO CREDIT ANSWER
The people at Walmart are friendlier.

8. Contrast the very worst that a capitalist "tyrant" can do to you (as a malcontented worker or an obnoxious customer) versus what a socialist tyrant can do to you.

SAMPLE FULL CREDIT ANSWER

A capitalist boss can at worst fire a worker or refuse to sell to a customer. In contrast, the socialist ruler can assign an enemy to grueling work in Siberia (or its equivalent), deny educational opportunities to his children, provide inadequate health care, etc.

SAMPLE PARTIAL CREDIT ANSWER

A capitalist boss can fire you, that's really it.

SAMPLE NO CREDIT ANSWER

The socialist can't calculate resource costs but the capitalist boss can.

The Failures of Socialism—History

Economic Theory and History

We are trying to walk a fine line in this chapter. On the one hand, it is important for the student to learn the historical record of many socialist governments. Conventional treatments (at least in the United States) typically focus on the atrocities of the African slave trade and the Jewish Holocaust under Nazi Germany, while completely omitting the atrocities committed by "leftist" governments.

On the other hand, we do not want to reinforce the common misconception—which we took great pains to dissect in Part I of the student text—that basic economic theory must be tested through empirical observation. Strictly speaking, economic theory by itself does not say, "If the government of a large country abolishes private ownership of the means of production, then millions of people will die."

Rather, economic theory claims that *other things equal,* abolition of private property will cripple the coordinating mechanism of market prices and the profit and loss test, and will also put great power in the hands of potentially wicked people. In principle, other factors could intervene, counteracting these forces. To give a silly example, Martians could show up and provide humans with solar-powered machines that produce consumer goods at the touch of a button. In this case, people's standard of living might rise after the switch to socialism, though it would be *in spite of* the switch, not *because* of it.

We are stressing this seemingly pedantic point because one of the standard arguments in favor of a mixed economy (as opposed to a command economy) is that the standard of living is obviously higher in the late twentieth century in Western countries compared to the late 19th century. The proponents of government intervention claim that this prosperity was the result of regulations imposed on a much more laissez-faire economy of the past. In other words, they argue that the growth of "big government" in the United States and other democratic nations went hand in hand with a growing economy. The proponent of free market economies would of course reply that 20th century economic growth would have been *even greater* had the Western governments limited their taxation and regulation.

If you want to learn more about the approach Mises took to economic theory and history, David Gordon's lecture (**http://mises.org/media/3978**) is an excellent starting place.

Communism versus Fascism

This is a course in economics, not political science or history. However, from an economic standpoint the standard political classification of various historical regimes is inadequate. Far from being polar opposites, the "far left" government of Stalinist Russia and the "far right" government of Hitler's Germany were very similar. Moreover, as we tried to explain in the last chapter as well as the current one, we can't compartmentalize "economic" and "personal" freedoms. If the government is the sole employer, then it has tremendous power over the individual. It's little consolation to have even a constitutionally protected "freedom to protest" if the government can assign you to work in Siberia and also controls all the media.

Socialism's Body Count

We do not want to commit the opposite mistake and give the impression that governments in countries that officially embrace capitalism are innocent of any wrongdoing. We have tried to be neutral in mentioning events from U.S. history, as some would defend (say) the atomic bombings of World War II as acts of self-defense which precluded even more deaths. The student should be aware, however, that modern socialists view capitalism as inherently imperialistic, and cite the frequent military actions of the United States as prime evidence.

The Broad Numbers

The Black Book of Communism is well-respected in academic circles and comes from Harvard University Press. We have opted for a small sample to give the student just a taste of the evidence of the brutal death toll of communism in the twentieth century.

Close to a Controlled Experiment

Again in this section, we explain that in the social sciences there can be no controlled experiment. But guided by our theoretical understanding of market versus command economies, the evidence seems compelling that State socialism is an inefficient economic system.

● ●

STUDY QUESTIONS

1. *Does the historical record *prove* that socialism is a flawed economic system?

No, because we can never know how history would have unfolded in an alternate timeline where socialism hadn't been implemented. (For an analogy, if someone has a headache and takes an aspirin, and then the headache gets worse, that doesn't prove that "aspirin makes your head hurt." It's probably the case that the headache would have gotten really bad had the person never taken an aspirin.)

2. What is wrong with the conventional "left / right" spectrum on which Stalin is the polar opposite of Hitler?

The problem is that economically speaking, the regimes of Stalin and Hitler were quite similar. Both involved heavy government involvement in the use of property, meaning that both regimes were the polar opposites of a pure market economy.

3. Do governments that officially support capitalism ever kill innocent people?

Yes, there are numerous examples of "anti-communist" authoritarian regimes that imprisoned and killed political opponents. If we broaden the category to include deaths of civilians living outside of the country, then the Western democracies (especially the United States and Great Britain) killed hundreds of thousands of civilians during the two world wars.

4. According to the text, which government massacred the largest number of civilians?

The Communist Chinese government.

5. *Explain this subsection title: "Close to a Controlled Experiment."**

There can never be a truly controlled experiment in the social sciences, because people learn from experience; thus the original experiment cannot be recreated, save for one minor adjustment. (This is the hallmark of a controlled experiment.) Even so, the examples of East and West Berlin, and especially North and South Korea, cast considerable doubt on the efficiency of socialism as an economic system.

Supplemental Materials

- Yuri Maltsev, "What Soviet Medicine Teaches Us," at **http://mises.org/daily/3650.**

  Maltsev earned his Ph.D. in economics in Moscow and served on a team of Soviet economists working on President Mikhail Gorbachev's policy of perestroika, before defecting to the United States. Maltsev is a champion of the market economy, and has powerful first-hand experience to justify his views. In this article he warns of government "solutions" to health care.

- Yuri Maltsev, "Farewell to Aleksandr Solzhenitsyn," at **http://mises.org/daily/3065.**

  In this article Maltsev explains the personal life and literary achievements of the Soviet dissident and Nobel laureate Aleksandr Solzhenitsyn, author of *The Gulag Archipelago.*

SUGGESTED ACTIVITIES

(1) Have the student scour news accounts of "right wing" and "left wing" governments or guerrilla groups, and try to isolate what the difference is supposed to be. Typically, both groups are in favor of having the government control property, it's just that the "right wing" groups want to redistribute wealth to the owners of multinational corporations, whereas the "left wing" groups want to redistribute wealth to rural peasants.

(2) Have the student peruse standard history texts or check the documentaries on the History Channel. There will probably be extensive coverage of the crimes of Nazi Germany, with relatively little (if any) attention paid to the much larger death toll at the hands of communist dictatorships.

Communist or Fascist? Place the letter of the correct conventional label next to each (in)famous government ruler.

A. communist   B. fascist

1. _____ Adolf Hitler   2. _____ Pol Pot

3. _____ Mao Tse-Tung   4. _____ Vladimir Lenin

5. _____ Benito Mussolini   6. _____ Joseph Stalin

Multiple Choice. Write the letter of the best answer to each question.

7. A system that seeks to establish government ownership over the means of production through a revolution in the working class.

   A. socialism
   B. communism
   C. capitalism
   D. fascism

8. A system that seeks to establish government control over the means of production while retaining the institution of private property.

   A. socialism
   B. communism
   C. capitalism
   D. fascism

9. Communism and Nazism are both forms of
    A. anarchism
    B. socialism
    C. entrepreneurism
    D. capitalism

10. Pol Pot's Khmer Rouge communist regime killed up to 25% of its own people in which country?
    A. Vietnam
    B. China
    C. North Korea
    D. Cambodia

11. "[O]ne particular feature of many Communist regimes [was] their systematic use of _____ as a weapon."
    A. famine
    B. gas
    C. poison
    D. disease
    E. Kalishnikovs

12. By far, which country's experience with communism cost the most lives?
    A. U.S.S.R
    B. North Korea
    C. People's Republic of China
    D. Vietnam

13. Post WWII, where in Europe was the contrast between relative capitalism and communism the starkest?

    A. Paris

    B. Berlin

    C. Warsaw

    D. Moscow

14. In nighttime satellite photographs, this communist country is distinguished by its darkness and its neighbors' brightness.

    A. North Korea

    B. People's Republic of China

    C. Japan

    D. Ukraine

Short Answer:
On the lines provided, answer the questions in 1 to 3 sentences.

15. Compare and contrast communism and fascism.

282 | Lessons for the Young Economist: Teacher's Manual

16. Explain how the conventional "Left Wing/Right Wing" dichotomy (or Left/Right Spectrum) with communists on the left and fascists on the right makes little sense in terms of economics.

_____

_____

_____

_____

_____

_____

_____

_____

_____

17. Does the material in this chapter show that we prove economic theory with experimental evidence?

_____

_____

_____

_____

_____

_____

_____

_____

_____

_____

Communist or Fascist?

a. communist   b. fascist

1. B	2. A	3. A
4. A	5. B	6. A

Multiple Choice:

7. B	8. D	9. B	10. D
11. A	12. C	13. B	14. A

Short Answer:

15. Compare and contrast communism and fascism.

SAMPLE FULL CREDIT ANSWER
Communism achieves total government control of the means of production through a workers' violent revolution. Fascism allows citizens to retain nominal ownership of factories, stores, etc., but it heavily regulates them to the point that they are merely following the government's orders. Historically communism focused on international class struggle while fascism tended to be nationalistic and racial.

SAMPLE PARTIAL CREDIT ANSWER
Under communism the government owns everything, but under fascism the government technically allows private owners who have to obey all the government's orders.

SAMPLE NO CREDIT ANSWER
Communism is left wing, fascism is right wing.

16. Explain how the conventional "Left Wing/Right Wing" dichotomy (or Left/Right Spectrum) with communists on the left and fascists on the right makes little sense in terms of economics.

SAMPLE FULL CREDIT ANSWER
Both communism (extreme left wing) and fascism (extreme right wing) are examples of socialism. It is more useful to group Stalinist Russia and Nazi Germany in the same category of totalitarianism, and contrast it with a society based on private property where government officials can't violate individual rights.

SAMPLE PARTIAL CREDIT ANSWER
Both are socialism.

SAMPLE NO CREDIT ANSWER
As bad as the fascists were, they didn't kill as many people as the communists did.

17. Does the material in this chapter show that we prove economic theory with experimental evidence?

SAMPLE FULL CREDIT ANSWER
No, we can never have a truly controlled experiment in economics. However, our deductive logic might give us true principles that, in practice, are insignificant and/or are swamped by other factors that we didn't include in our reasoning. Looking at history is thus a useful "check" on our principles or laws.

SAMPLE PARTIAL CREDIT ANSWER
No, we are just seeing if our economic laws are illustrated in history.

SAMPLE NO CREDIT ANSWER
Yes, the 20th century clearly proves the laws of economics.

Part IV

INTERVENTIONISM: THE MIXED ECONOMY

Price Controls

The Vision of Interventionism

I n this final portion of the book, we focus on major components of the "mixed economy." Most intellectuals recognize
(at long last, in some cases) that pure socialism doesn't work.
However, they are still unwilling to embrace a society with
complete private property rights. They reject both pure socialism and pure capitalism, and opt for a third way, an interventionist system that (allegedly) avoids the unseemly excesses of
a pure market while stopping short of outright central planning.

Much of the analysis in this section of the book is comparable to what is found in mainstream textbooks, though the
emphasis would be different. In a standard text, for example,
much space would be devoted to diagrammatic expositions of
the "welfare losses" arising from interventions such as tariffs.
In this course we do not dwell on the graphs, which leaves us
more space to analyze the various topics in greater detail.

Price Ceilings

The analysis in this section is fairly straightforward. We
offer just a few comments to help you allocate your time.

Immediate Shortages

Immediate shortages are the most critical consequence of price ceilings. For students wishing to go on in economics, make sure they know how to use supply and demand curves to illustrate the shortage.

Lower Supply in the Long Run

In addition to an immediate reduction in the quantity supplied in the short run, price ceilings also reduce the supply in the long run. For advanced students, you can point out the subtlety here: The price ceiling moves output *along* the original supply curve to the bottom left (yielding a smaller quantity supplied), but it actually moves the entire *supply curve* to the left over time, relative to where the supply curve would have been in the absence of the price ceiling.

To give an exaggerated illustration: If the government suddenly declared that apartments could only rent for $1 per month, the quantity supplied would fall sharply. Most owners would only "rent" to their friends and out-of-town relatives, and would use their remaining rooms as storage. (They might rent it out as storage space if this evaded the rent control law.) Some might be more philanthrophic and allow tenants to move in who had passed some other test of merit, such as rehabilitated drug abusers or ex-cons trying to get back on their feet. However, if the government removed the price control after only a few months, the quantity supplied could quickly snap back to its original level, just as soon as the contracts for the existing tenants expired.

On the other hand, if the government kept the $1 price ceiling in place for a few *decades* before removing it, the quantity supplied would not quickly return to its original level (let alone the level it would have achieved if there had been no price ceiling in the intervening decades). This is because the landlords would not have replaced their deteriorating buildings. In fact, once they were sure the rent control law was going to last, many landlords would have had their apartment buildings bulldozed and replaced them with stores or parking garages. The lesson is that the absurd price ceiling of $1 per month would initially suppress the quantity supplied, but eventually it would also restrict the entire supply curve. After having an absurd $1 per month ceiling in place for decades, if the government suddenly removed the control and allowed the market to set prices, there wouldn't be many physical apartment units in existence at that moment, no matter how high the market price soared after the removal of the ceiling.

Non-price Rationing

One of the functions of the (undisturbed) market price is that it rations the available supply of a good among the competing demands for it. In essence, if someone wants more units of the good, he has to bid more dollars for it. This of course strikes many observers as unfair, since it gives an obvious advantage to the wealthy.

However, by placing a cap on the price, the government doesn't eliminate the fact of scarcity; there are still more people who want to use the good, than there are units of the good to go around. All that happens is that the rationing must occur through *non-price* mechanisms. This actually might end up being more distasteful to the proponents of the price control, than the original price rationing.

For example, under rent control landlords can be much pickier in which tenants they select for their available apartments. They might insist on seeing several months' worth of paycheck stubs, run a background check on the applicant, and require letters of reference from previous landlords. They might also prefer tenants who travel in the same social circles, or come from the same ethnic group, whether from outright bias or because they subconsciously feel more comfortable letting someone move into the building when (say) he goes to the same church. In such an environment, ethnic minorities and recent immigrants—especially if they don't speak the native tongue—will be at a huge disadvantage, and may find it very difficult to find a place to live. This outcome is the exact *opposite* of what most proponents of rent control desire.

Drop in Quality

Be sure the student understands that even the ostensible winners from price ceilings are not as lucky as the first stage of the analysis suggests. In other words, even the tenants who receive a break on their rent may end up with lousier service from the landlord.

Price Floors

As with the previous section, the analysis here is straightforward.

Immediate Surplus (or Glut)

Be sure the student understands that price floors cause immediate surpluses (or gluts); this is the most important consequence. The student planning to go on in economics should also be able to graphically illustrate a price floor and the corresponding surplus.

Lower Demand in the Long Run

The analysis here is the mirror-image of the effects of price ceilings on supply. In the case of price floors, the immediate effect is a restriction in the quantity demanded. That is, the artificially high price moves along the original demand curve (up and to the left). But over time, the price floor (and the associated higher-than-equilibrium price) leads the buyers to adapt by reducing their dependence on the good or service in question. The result can be a leftward shift in the entire demand curve, so that even if the price floor were suddenly removed, a wage (price) at the original, lower level would not draw forth the same quantity demanded.

Non-wage Competition

One way of illustrating the consequences in this subsection is to point out the different unemployment rates based on various demographics. (As of this writing, the Bureau of Labor Statistics has links to such data at the bottom of this link: **http://www.bls.gov/cps/#data**.) The very groups who are the most economically vulnerable tend to have the highest unemployment rates, and one of the explanations is that these groups are legally forbidden from underbidding other workers who are earning the minimum wage. Proponents of the legislation would argue that it is indecent for someone to make less than the minimum wage, but it's arguably more indecent for someone to be willing to work but unable to find a job.

Drop in Workplace Quality

By forcing employers to pay more per hour, and by ensuring a long line of willing workers ready to replace anyone who quits, minimum wage laws reduce the incentive for employers to make jobs attractive in other dimensions. For example, the employer might reduce break times, stop providing free food in the lunch room, and set the thermostat higher in the summer and lower in the winter. The employer might be slower to replace overhead fluorescent bulbs, and (in an office environment) might spend less money on office furniture. Perhaps the bathrooms will be stocked with very cheap toilet paper and clinical-smelling hand soap.

• •

STUDY QUESTIONS

1. What is "mixed" in the term *mixed economy*?

A mixed economy combines features of both capitalism and socialism, namely private ownership and government direction.

2. How can the quantity supplied of apartments fall, even in the short run? Isn't there a fixed number of apartment units at any given time?

Remember that the quantity supplied means the number of apartment units *offered for rent*. As the legally permissible price falls, more and more owners won't find it worthwhile to go through the hassle and risk of renting their physically available rooms to total strangers.

3. How might price ceilings on gasoline impede the evacuation of a city in the path of an oncoming hurricane?

At any given time, gasoline stations in a typical city don't have enough fuel in the underground tanks to withstand a mass exodus of the entire population, with every motorist filling up before leaving town. If the authorities impose price ceilings to prevent "gouging" after the news breaks, the stations will run out of gas before everyone has had a chance to refuel. Consequently some motorists will be stranded on the interstates, impeding traffic flow.

4. *How can minimum wage laws reduce the long-run demand (not just short-run quantity demanded) for labor?

Business owners may respond to a minimum wage law by buying more machines and redesigning their workplaces to operate with a fewer number of higher-skilled employees. Once businesses have adapted in this fashion, the demand curve for labor will have shifted to the left, because even at the original wage level, businesses would now demand a lower quantity.

5. How can a minimum wage actually hurt even the workers who stay on the job?

Employers could reduce workplace amenities and other perks to compensate for the higher labor expenses. It is possible that employees would actually prefer the original combination of pay and other benefits to the combination they receive after the imposition of the minimum wage.

Supplemental Materials

- Henry Hazlitt, *Economics In One Lesson*, Chapters XVIII and XIX.

    As with all of Hazlitt's chapters, these provide a wonderful yet succinct analysis.

- Gene Callahan, *Economics For Real People*, Chapters 11–12.

    Callahan provides a good exposition on the problems with price controls, from an Austrian perspective.

- Robert Murphy, "The Gas-Line Quagmire in Iraq," at **http:// mises.org/daily/2026**.

    Murphy applies the lessons of economic theory to the real-world example of long gas lines in post-invasion Iraq.

- Bloomberg story on Hugo Chavez imposing price controls after devaluing the currency: **http://www.bloomberg.com/apps/ne ws?pid=newsarchive&sid=aTtr11jqdrdM**

    This news story actually combines two different issues. Hugo Chavez first devalued Venezuela's currency on certain foreign transactions, so that the bolivar would exchange for fewer U.S. dollars. (Many speculate that Chavez's motivation was to earn more revenue—when quoted in bolivars—from selling Venezuela's surplus oil on the world market.) The devaluation meant that Venezuelan merchants who relied on foreign imports of the affected goods saw their expenses instantly rise. Yet Chavez declared it illegal for the merchants to raise the prices they charged their customers in turn. (You could ask the student to do some online research to see if any shortages were reported in Venezuela following Chavez's new policies.)

- Peter Schiff on Samoan price controls: **http://www.youtube. com/watch?v=_LaPGIIAyk4**

    Investment manager Peter Schiff is considered a hero in certain circles for his uncanny predictions of the housing collapse. (A compilation of some of his TV forecasts can be seen at **http://www.youtube. com/watch?v=ZOYTY5TWtmU.**) In the above clip he discusses the interesting example of Samoan price controls and how they destroyed an industry.

- Walter Block, debate on minimum wage against Jared Bernstein, audio at **http://mises.org/media/2452**.

    Austrian economist and libertarian writer Walter Block debates the minimum wage on a radio program with progressive economist Jared Bernstein.

- Joe Salerno, "Case Studies in Price Controls," audio at **http:// mises.org/media/2076**.

    Salerno provides interesting historical examples to illustrate the theoretical points in this chapter.

SUGGESTED ACTIVITIES

(1) Often a good way to introduce the problems with the minimum wage—especially with someone who initially thinks it's a good idea—is to ask, "Why not set a minimum wage of $100 per hour, so everyone would be rich?" (The same thing could be done for rent control of $10 per month.) Another way to approach the issue is to ask, "Why doesn't every worker—including brain surgeons and star quarterbacks—get paid the minimum wage?"

(2) While on an interstate road trip, have the student find out the minimum wage levels applicable in each state along the route using Wikipedia: http://en.wikipedia.org/wiki/List_of_U.S._minimum_wages. Then pay attention to how many workers the various restaurants have along the way, trying to hold other factors constant (such as time of day, weekday versus weekend, size of the crowd, etc.). For example, as of this writing the minimum wage in Washington state was $8.55 for workers 16 and older, whereas in adjacent Idaho it was only $7.25. Other things equal, we would expect to see fewer workers at fast-food restaurants in Washington. (Be careful if stopping at a fancier restaurant, because minimum wage laws usually make exceptions for workers who earn tips.)

Short Answer:
On the lines provided, answer the questions in 1 to 3 sentences.

1. Explain how interventionists vie for "the best of both worlds."

_____

_____

_____

_____

_____

_____

_____

2. Why would someone support a price ceiling?

_____

_____

_____

_____

_____

_____

_____

_____

3. The textbook claims that price ceilings (a) cause immediate short-ages and (b) lower long-run supply. What's the difference? Use a specific example to illustrate.

_____

_____

_____

_____

_____

_____

_____

_____

_____

_____

4. Explain why minimum wage laws lead to higher unemployment rates.

_____

_____

_____

_____

_____

_____

_____

_____

_____

_____

5. Explain how the poorest and most desperate are actually hurt by minimum wage laws.

_____

_____

_____

_____

_____

_____

_____

_____

_____

6. Explain how minimum wage laws might lead to a decline in workplace quality.

_____

_____

_____

_____

_____

_____

_____

_____

_____

_____

Short Answer:

1. Explain how interventionists vie for "the best of both worlds."

SAMPLE FULL CREDIT ANSWER
The interventionists want to retain a market economy with private property, but have the government selectively "intervene" in order to correct certain features they dislike. Thus, the interventionists claim they are avoiding the excesses of pure capitalism and the horrors of pure socialism.

SAMPLE PARTIAL CREDIT ANSWER
The interventionists want a mixed system that is better than capitalism and socialism.

SAMPLE NO CREDIT ANSWER
The interventionists take cues from historians as well as economists.

2. Why would someone support a price ceiling?

SAMPLE FULL CREDIT ANSWER
Someone might support a price ceiling, thinking that this will help keep certain things affordable. For example, someone might support a price ceiling on apartments or baby food, so that poor people can access shelter and feed their infants.

SAMPLE PARTIAL CREDIT ANSWER
To help the poor.

SAMPLE NO CREDIT ANSWER
To make more profit.

3. The textbook claims that price ceilings (a) cause immediate short-ages and (b) lower long-run supply. What's the difference? Use a specific example to illustrate.

SAMPLE FULL CREDIT ANSWER
A price ceiling pushes down the price from its equilibrium level, moving along the original supply curve to a lower quantity sup-plied (and a higher quantity demanded). This is the immediate shortage, for example a million people might try to find apart-ments but only 800,000 are offered on the market. In the long run, investors don't build as many new apartment buildings because of the price ceiling, so that the whole supply curve of apartments shifts to the left, or at least doesn't shift to the right as much as it otherwise would have.

SAMPLE PARTIAL CREDIT ANSWER
A price ceiling pushes us along the original supply curve in the short run, and moves the supply curve in the long run.

SAMPLE NO CREDIT ANSWER
Price ceilings cause unsold inventory to pile up, disturbing equilib-rium.

4. Explain why minimum wage laws lead to higher unemployment rates.

SAMPLE FULL CREDIT ANSWER
Minimum wage laws are set above the market-clearing level, meaning that the quantity of labor supplied by workers is higher than the quantity demanded by employers. This means some workers can't get hired, even though they want to work at prevail-ing wage rates. This is the typical definition of unemployment.

SAMPLE PARTIAL CREDIT ANSWER
Minimum wage laws make some workers too expensive to hire.

SAMPLE NO CREDIT ANSWER
They make workers unable to find jobs.

5. Explain how the poorest and most desperate are actually hurt by minimum wage laws.

SAMPLE FULL CREDIT ANSWER
Immigrants and low-skilled workers can only compete by offering to do jobs at lower wages than native and high-skilled workers. Minimum wage laws make it illegal for them to undercut their rivals too much. Minimum wage laws effectively take away the one option that the poor and desperate have, to ensure that they can get a job.

SAMPLE PARTIAL CREDIT ANSWER
High-skilled workers can get hired above the minimum wage, so it doesn't directly affect their working conditions.

SAMPLE NO CREDIT ANSWER
Nobody can really live on the minimum wage, so it hardly helps the poorest workers who rely on it.

6. Explain how minimum wage laws might lead to a decline in workplace quality.

SAMPLE FULL CREDIT ANSWER
Employers attract workers through a combination of job features including salary (or wage), health benefits, length of lunch breaks, temperature of the workplace, etc. If minimum wage laws force an employer to offer higher monetary compensation than he otherwise would have, he might cut back on some of the other desirable features of the job to recoup the money.

SAMPLE PARTIAL CREDIT ANSWER
The employer might pay the higher wages by cutting back elsewhere, such as air conditioning.

SAMPLE NO CREDIT ANSWER
It can lower workplace morale if employees are paid too little.

LESSON 18

Sales and Income Taxes

Government Spending

In the introduction to this lesson, we adopt the position of Ludwig von Mises when it came to the "value-free" analysis of government intervention: Mises believed that economic science per se was objective and dispassionate; it could not say whether a sales tax was a good thing or a bad thing. However, in order for citizens to make informed decisions regarding important issues such as taxes, they needed economics to show them the full consequences of their decisions.

For some reason, standard economics texts do not typically discuss the obvious point that government spending necessarily diverts resources into channels where they otherwise would not have gone. In contrast, standard texts will devote inordinate amounts of time to discussing the "incidence" of particular taxes, depending on the relative elasticities of supply and demand. (For example, if the government levies a sales tax on cigarettes, the consumers will end up bearing the brunt of the tax, whereas a comparable sales tax on Pepsi would probably fall heavily on the company, as Pepsi drinkers would shift into Coke.)

305

But when it comes to the issue of what governments *do* with their tax revenue, most economics books fail to mention the points we make in this opening section. Our observations here are not unique to the Austrian School; other free market economists have made them as well. For example, Milton Friedman said that the true burden of government should be measured by how much it *spends*, not how much it taxes. Friedman's observation is very relevant to the discussion here.

To clarify the examples in the student text: We bring up the example of Disneyland to make sure the student understands the way firms in the private sector overcome the problems we are attributing to political programs. In other words, we are showing why private spending by businesses doesn't misdirect resources—or rather, why there is a built-in penalty for private misdirection—the way government spending does.

How Government Finances Its Spending

It is a staple of the free-market economics tradition that government revenues must come from taxation, deficits (borrowing), and/or inflation. So be sure that the student understands these three methods, and sees how the public ultimately ends up paying for government spending regardless of how it is financed. (The appeal of borrowing and inflation is that the politicians can *appear* to deliver popular spending programs today, without a corresponding expense. But this appearance is deceptive.) Note that the discussions of deficits and inflation are deferred to later lessons in the book.

We stress this in the text, but it bears repeating here: The government distorts the private economy twice, first when it sucks out revenue, and second when it spends its funds. The exaggerated example of a 200% income tax tries to isolate the two effects. At such an absurd tax rate, the government would raise little if any tax revenue, and if it limited itself to spending tax revenues, even government spending would be very small. Yet it would be wrong to conclude that this hypothetical government didn't distort the economy very much; the draconian 200% income tax rate would virtually wipe out the official economy and drive productive activities either out of existence or into the black market. (Note that in this example, Friedman's suggestion of focusing on government spending as the measure of government's burden would be misleading.)

Sales Taxes

To repeat, in a standard undergraduate economics text, they will typically analyze sales taxes with the aim of understanding the "incidence," meaning whether the consumers or the producers bear the brunt of a new tax. In these standard textbooks, there *is* a discussion of the general loss to the economy in the form of a "deadweight loss." The idea here is that when the government makes goods and services artificially expensive, potential trades do not occur, so that the gains from trade among producers and consumers are reduced. We have tried to get across the same idea in the student text, without using the actual term *deadweight loss* and without recourse to supply and demand graphs.

Income Taxes

Depending on your own judgment, you may wish to spend more or less time on the issues of tax brackets, tax-deductible expenses versus tax-exempt income, and so forth. For many students, these are vague phrases that don't really become significant until they purchase their own houses and the tax code has personal consequences. It is probably worth clearing up two common misconceptions, which are: (1) people can allegedly be hurt by a pay raise because it puts them in a higher tax bracket, and (2) businesses don't mind buying things that are "tax writeoffs." These views are false, though there is a grain of truth to them. (Specifically, a pay raise is not as advantageous when the marginal dollars are taxed at a high rate, and a business will not watch its expenses as carefully if they are tax deductible. But this is different from saying a person literally is hurt by a pay raise, or that a business actually makes money by increasing its expenses.)

The final example in the text illustrates the point that incentives do affect behavior. High income tax rates definitely distort the labor market. The distortion is not necessarily that highly productive people leave the labor market, but rather that they are guided more by non-pecuniary factors and in that respect the guidance provided by other people's spending is muted.

• •

STUDY QUESTIONS

1. *Does economics conclude that government spending is bad?

No, economics simply points out that resources will be directed to different projects when the government spends money. The goods and services produced because of government spending come at the expense of other goods and services that now will never exist. Economics per se can't say that one pattern of output is better or worse than the other, but it reminds us that there is a tradeoff, an opportunity cost to the government's actions.

2. How do we know that government spending diverts resources from the private sector? Does it matter how the government obtained its funds?

We know government spending diverts resources, because we can see that actual resources are consumed (or at least devoted to a specific end) when the government spends money. Those resources can't physically be used for private projects (at least in most cases). At this level of analysis, it doesn't matter how the government obtained its funds; its spending necessarily commits resources to particular projects and thereby makes them unavailable for entrepreneurs in the private sector.

3. **If the government builds a library, do we know that the private sector wouldn't have built a library instead?

This is a subtle question. Generally speaking, we can say that the government directs resources in different ways from how the private sector would; otherwise, there would be no point to government programs. However, it doesn't follow that entire categories of government services (such as old-age pensions or "free" libraries) exist in a vacuum left by the private sector. If the government didn't build any libraries—and especially if it lowered taxes accordingly by the amount it currently spends on libraries—then charitable groups would probably develop an alternative in the voluntary market sector. The market-produced "free" libraries would probably be much more modest in terms of the physical structures, especially in urban areas with high real estate prices, but it's likely that they would be more useful to their actual customers. At the very least, they would provide more useful services *per dollar spent*.

4. If the government raises a modest amount of money through taxation, do we know that the tax burden is light?

Not necessarily, as the example of a 200% income tax shows.

5. As long as people continue working, does the income tax have little effect on the economy?

Not necessarily, as the example of a worker considering a job in New York City shows.

Supplemental Materials

- Thomas DiLorenzo, "Rothbard's Economics of Taxation," audio at **http://mises.org/media/1324**.

    This is a self-explanatory lecture. If the student is going to read Rothbard's selection below, he or she would definitely benefit from first listening to DiLorenzo place the material in context.

- Hans Hoppe, "The Economics of Taxation," first two sections, at **http://mises.org/daily/2061**.

    Hoppe's treatment is compatible with the discussion in the student text. He shows that the classical economists (such as J.B. Say, after whom "Say's Law" is named) understood that one of the essential characteristics of taxation is its coercive nature. Ironically, most modern economics texts do not really dwell on this difference between taxation and, say, income earned voluntarily in the private sector. The point is not simply one of morality; we are not making a "mere" value judgment. As Hoppe shows, there are definite implications from organizing resource allocation on the basis of voluntary exchanges versus coercive transfers from citizens to the government. Part of the difference in perspective is no doubt due to the Austrian focus on the institution of private property and the role it plays in society.

- Murray Rothbard, *Man, Economy, and State*, pp. 914–27.

    Rothbard spells out the basics for a praxeological analysis of taxation. In other words, Rothbard uses the same theoretical framework that Mises had developed for the study of purposeful action when restricted to a market economy, and Rothbard applies it to the study of purposeful actions involving coercion. In this selection Rothbard looks at the specific category of coercion

involving "binary interventions," meaning cases where
one party takes resources from another. (In contrast
a price control would involve more than two parties,
since the government official interferes with exchanges
between two other people.) Taxation is just such a binary
intervention.

SUGGESTED ACTIVITIES

(1) The next time you are at a gas station, point out the sign indicating that the posted price includes all applicable sales taxes. Ask the student to guess how much of the pump price is due to federal and state sales taxes. Then show the actual answer here: **http://tonto.eia.doe. gov/energyexplained/index.cfm?page=gasoline_ factors_affecting_prices**.

(2) Explain to the student that the current incarnation of the federal income tax was enacted in 1913 through the Sixteenth Amendment: **http://en.wikipedia.org/wiki/ Sixteenth_Amendment_to_the_United_States_ Constitution**. Explain that when the tax was first enacted, the top rate was 7.0%, applicable to people earning $500,000 or more. (Note that this much income in 1913 would be equivalent to more than $10 million in income in 2010.) Point out to the student that obviously, tax rates have increased since the income tax was first enacted. Ask the student to guess (a) the top tax rate on income in U.S. history and (b) what the top tax rate was in 1918, five years after the initial 7% rate. Then have the student examine the actual history here: **http://taxfoundation. org/taxdata/show/151.html#fed_individual_rate_ history-20091231**. (Start at the bottom of the document and scroll upward.)

Short Answer:
On the lines provided, answer the questions in 1 to 3 sentences.

1. Discuss the difference in economic efficiency between Disney spending $10 million to improve Disneyland and the government spending $10 million to build a bomber.

_____

_____

_____

_____

_____

_____

_____

2. Explain why political authorities in an interventionist economy cannot objectively measure how much their citizens benefit from their expenditures.

_____

_____

_____

_____

_____

_____

_____

_____

_____

3. Sometimes the government spends money to build something (e.g., a library) because entrepreneurs won't do it themselves. Does this prove that the government spending is a good thing?

4. Identify the three typical methods by which governments raise money.

5. Explain why high sales tax rates fuel black markets.

6. Suppose that there are two income tax brackets. Income up to $100,000 is taxed at 10 percent, while income higher than that is taxed at 2%. Mary originally earns $99,000, but then gets a raise and now earns $101,000. How much total tax does Mary owe the government in each scenario? Has the raise pushed Mary into a higher tax bracket? If so, is she worse off (assuming she only cares about her take-home salary)?

_____

_____

_____

_____

_____

_____

_____

_____

_____

_____

_____

_____

_____

_____

_____

_____

_____

_____

_____

Short Answer:

1. Discuss the difference in economic efficiency between Disney spending $10 million to improve Disneyland and the government spending $10 million to build a bomber.

SAMPLE FULL CREDIT ANSWER
Disney is guided by profit and loss. Its executives are only spending the money because they think consumers will value the improvements more than the expense, meaning that resources will be tend to be efficiently used. In contrast, the government has no idea how much extra value the public gets from an additional bomber, and therefore has no guidance on whether it is spending tax dollars wisely.

SAMPLE PARTIAL CREDIT ANSWER
The government gets no feedback on its spending.

SAMPLE NO CREDIT ANSWER
Bombers are more important than amusement park rides and so should get priority.

2. Explain why political authorities in an interventionist economy cannot objectively measure how much their citizens benefit from their expenditures.

SAMPLE FULL CREDIT ANSWER
Most government services are paid out of general revenues, which are taken involuntarily from the citizens. Then, the services are often provided with a low or zero price. The citizens' desires for resources to go into one area versus another are thus virtually ignored.

SAMPLE PARTIAL CREDIT ANSWER
The government doesn't have real competition, so the public has to take whatever it gives them.

SAMPLE NO CREDIT ANSWER
Since value is subjective, we can't ever really know if we are using resources efficiently.

3. Sometimes the government spends money to build something (e.g., a library) because entrepreneurs won't do it themselves. Does this prove that the government spending is a good thing?

SAMPLE FULL CREDIT ANSWER
No, because we aren't seeing the opportunity cost of the project. The resources going into the library would otherwise have produced different goods and services that the consumers valued more (since the private sector wouldn't have built the library on its own). If the library were a gift from Martians, it would be valuable, but it isn't worth the potential goods and services that now will never be produced.

SAMPLE PARTIAL CREDIT ANSWER
No, because people in the private sector could've built something else.

SAMPLE NO CREDIT ANSWER
Yes, because literacy is crucial for democracy.

4. Identify the three typical methods by which governments raise money.

Taxation, borrowing, and inflation.

5. Explain why high sales tax rates fuel black market economies.

SAMPLE FULL CREDIT ANSWER
The high sales tax rate gives an incentive for sellers and buyers to keep transactions "off the books" or "under the table." By hiding sales, the participants don't have to report the transaction and therefore don't pay the tax. This allows both buyer and seller to walk away with more money than if they had complied with the tax code.

SAMPLE PARTIAL CREDIT ANSWER
People hide their transactions to escape the tax.

SAMPLE NO CREDIT ANSWER
Sales taxes reduce consumption and encourage saving.

6. Suppose that there are two income tax brackets. Income up to $100,000 is taxed at 10 percent, while income higher than that is taxed at 20 percent. Mary originally earns $99,000, but then gets a raise and now earns $101,000. How much total tax does Mary owe the government in each scenario? Has the raise pushed Mary into a higher tax bracket? If so, is she worse off (assuming she only cares about her take-home salary)?

Originally Mary pays 10% x $99,000 = $9,900 in tax. After her raise, she pays (10% x $100,000) + (20% x $1,000) = $10,000 + $200 = $10,200 in tax. Yes, the raise pushed her into the higher tax bracket. No, Mary isn't worse off, because originally her take-home salary was $99,000 - $9,900 = $89,100, but after her raise it's $101,000 - $10,200 = $90,800.

Tariffs and Quotas

Mercantilism

The case for free trade is simultaneously one of the most difficult to convey to skeptics, and yet endorsed by the vast majority of economists. Not merely "free market economists," but even many otherwise interventionist economists, understand the mutual benefits when countries reduce trade barriers and liberalize imports and exports.

There is a vast literature for the non-expert on the topic of free trade. Obviously we could not summarize every argument in the student text, and we couldn't cite every relevant reading below in the Supplemental Materials. But if the student is interested, you can pursue the topic much further than some of the other ones in this course. The case for free trade is crucial to understanding markets generally, and so extra time spent on this topic will not be wasted.

We open the discussion by explaining mercantilism. Make sure the student recognizes that although mercantilism as an official doctrine has long been discredited, it obviously survives in both government policies and the popular understanding of trade. The only real change over the centuries is that nowadays, the emphasis is not on the accumulation of gold and silver, but instead on domestic "job creation."

The General Case for Free Trade

The arguments in this section should be self-explanatory. To help you explain some of the nuances, here are two clarifying notes:

First, you should realize that Adam Smith didn't present the modern case for free trade. What Smith really did was show that if two countries have *absolute* advantages in different goods, then both countries grow richer by specializing in those goods and trading with each other. The more general case, in which even a country that has the absolute advantage in everything can still gain from trading with a less productive neighbor, is typically credited to David Ricardo (though some historians of economic thought question whether he invented the idea). (There is a numerical illustration in the Suggested Activities below.)

Second, you should be aware of the distinction between a *trade deficit* and a *current account deficit*. This distinction will probably not be important for most students, but especially if you try to make analogies between individual households and countries, knowing the distinction may help you keep things straight (at least in your own mind). A trade deficit occurs when Country A buys more goods and services from Country B than vice versa. People often describe this situation by saying that Country A is "living beyond its means."

However, this can be inaccurate because a current account deficit occurs when Country A spends more on goods and services sold by Country B, than Country A *earns in income* from the people in Country B. Now if the only source of income were through current sales of goods and services, a trade deficit and a current account deficit would be equivalent. But in the real world, what can happen is that, say, people in Country A in the year 2010 buy $1 billion worth of stock in corporations located in Country B. Then in the year 2011, those corporations issue $50 million worth of dividends to the stockholders who live in Country A. These stockholders can then spend the money on goods and services produced in Country B, and in a sense will just "recycle the money" back to Country B. If these were the only transactions, Country A would still have a $50 million trade deficit with Country B, but it would have a $0 current account deficit. There would be nothing "unsustainable" about the people in Country A receiving an annual influx of goods and services from Country B, which would represent their annual earnings on the $1 billion investment made back in the year 2010.

These nuances are probably beyond the scope of most students' abilities, but you should be aware of them. For example, if you try to explain that a country running a trade deficit is analogous to a household that consumes more than it produces, you should realize that a retired person doesn't produce anything. Yet if he has saved up enough during his working years, he can comfortably run "trade deficits" with the rest of the community for decades after he has quit working. It's even possible that his net worth continues to grow after retirement, just so long as he consumes less than the investment earnings each year. To sum up, just as a retired person can derive an income from previous investments, and thus he "consumes more than he produces" year after year, so too can Country A run perpetual trade deficits with Country B, so long as Country A is using the income it earns from previous investments in assets located in Country B.

(Note that the distinction we have drawn between income earned by "producing" with one's labor versus income earned from financial assets is arguably spurious; the successful stock speculator is a "producer" just as much as the farmer, from a certain point of view. We are just warning you that the way trade statistics are calculated, a "trade deficit" narrowly refers to cross-country exchanges of conventional goods and services, rather than capturing every conceivable way a person in Country A could earn income from a person in Country B.)

Tariffs

There are numerous ways that free-market economists have tried to show the flaws of protectionism, i.e., the philosophy of using tariffs (or other trade barriers) to "protect" domestic workers. You may want to first read all of the Supplemental Materials before teaching this topic, to familiarize yourself with the various arguments and styles.

As we stated in the student text, it actually concedes too much to the protectionist position to "follow the money"; it's a bad habit that often leads to faulty conclusions. Yet Hazlitt and others have focused on dollar expenditures simply to pinpoint precisely where the protectionist goes wrong. In other words, if no one had ever uttered fallacious protectionist arguments, we probably wouldn't even talk about dollars going into different sectors. Rather, we would explain that trade barriers divert resources into less efficient sectors, and lower total output. Therefore trade barriers make everyone in the world poorer, on average.

Import Quotas

As the text explains, tariffs and import quotas can be quite similar in their broad effects on domestic employment and consumers. (One *difference* is that under a tariff, government collects more revenue, whereas under a quota the foreign producer can keep the higher earnings on the artificially restricted number of units sold in the country.)

The last point we make in the text is that a quota can potentially cause far more damage than a tariff, simply because the government could impose a draconian quota without it being as obvious as if the government imposed a comparable tariff. Especially with the passage of time, the effects of a quota become harder to gauge, since we would have to know what the free-trade level of imports would be. For example, if Country A originally imported 100,000 cars from Country B, and then Country A's government imposed a 90,000-vehicle quota, that would probably be equivalent to a significant but not outrageous tariff rate. However, as the years passed, the original 90,000-vehicle quota would become more and more onerous. This is because, in the absence of the quota, the number of imports would probably have grown over the years.

• •

STUDY QUESTIONS

1. *Could every government successfully implement mercantilist policies?

No, because it's impossible for every country to run a trade surplus with every other country. In contrast, the argument for free trade *can* apply to all countries; every government can consistently enrich its own citizens by enacting free trade policies.

2. What historical role did Adam Smith play with respect to mercantilism?

Adam Smith showed that a country impoverishes itself if it tries to produce at home, what could be purchased abroad more cheaply. Smith's arguments focused on the logic of absolute advantage, where each country was best at producing at least one particular good. In that setting, it naturally made sense for all countries to specialize in those goods in which they had the absolute advantage.

3. Explain the meaning (not the cause) of this statement: "The U.S. ran a trade deficit with Japan last year."

During the course of the previous year, people in the United States spent more money on goods and services produced in Japan, than the people in Japan spent on goods and services produced in the United States.

4. Explain: "The economic case for free trade is unilateral."

If Country A and B initially have tariff barriers erected against each other, Country A grows richer by lowering its own tariffs *even if* Country B doesn't reciprocate. In other words, the benefit of a free trade agreement is *not* simply that lowering your own barriers gives your diplomats leverage when they try to convince other governments into reducing barriers against exports from your own country.

5. Explain: "A tariff doesn't increase employment, it just rearranges it."

So long as wages are allowed to adjust, workers can always find employment in the market economy. When a tariff causes employment to expand in a particular sector, therefore, this doesn't "create jobs" on net, but merely sucks workers out of other sectors.

Supplemental Materials

- Frédéric Bastiat, "Petition of the Candlemakers," at **http://bastiat.org/en/petition.html**.

  This is one of the most famous economics essays of all time. It is (of course) a satirical play on standard mercantilist arguments. Bastiat "proves" that shutting out "unfair" competition from the sun would be a great boon for industry.

- Henry Hazlitt, *Economics In One Lesson*, Chapters XI–XII.

  Hazlitt continues in the great tradition of economists showing the absurdities of protectionist arguments. Hazlitt picks apart the standard case for trade barriers and shows the importance of focusing on the "unseen."

- Robert Murphy, "People *Can* Just Get Along," at **http://mises.org/daily/1684**.

  A self-explanatory essay on the gains from trade, as well as a treatment of some modern objections.

SUGGESTED ACTIVITIES

Especially for the student who will study economics at higher levels, you may wish to go over the following numerical example which illustrates comparative advantage in the case of international trade. (This example was drawn from the class notes for an introductory undergrad class in macroeconomics.)

Suppose that the following table summarizes the physical productivities of U.S. and Mexican workers in two different industries:

U.S.	MEXICO
2 TVs / worker day	1 TV / worker day
5 DVDs / worker day	2 DVDs / worker day

The U.S. workers have the *absolute* advantage in both lines, because 2 > 1 and 5 > 2. However, the U.S. workers have the *comparative* advantage only in DVD production, because (5/2) > (2/1). To see it another way, the U.S. workers can make twice as many TVs per day as their Mexican counterparts, but can make more than twice as many DVDs per day.

Intuitively, we know (recall our discussion of comparative advantage in the case of Marcia and John in Lesson 8) that if the U.S. specializes in DVDs and Mexico in TVs, the people of both countries will have more consumption opportunities and hence will be better off in material terms. But in order to drive home the point, let's pick some simple numbers to illustrate the process from the point of view of individual firms and workers. Note that these numbers are *illustrative* only; there is nothing magical about these particular values, they are serving as examples to give a concrete illustration of the general principle.

U.S. IN AUTARKY (BEFORE TRADE)

TV price is $50 each, DVD price is $20 each, and workers get paid $100 / day.

Note that this is consistent with the table above. A U.S. worker can make 2 TVs per day, thus earning $100 in revenue for his employer. In a competitive labor market, the worker therefore earns $100 per day. Or, if the worker goes to the DVD plant, he cranks out 5 units per day, again yielding $100 in revenue for his employer.

MEXICO IN AUTARKY

TV price is $10 each, DVD price is $5 each, and workers get paid $10 / day.

Note that these numbers are also consistent with the table above. A worker can yield his employer either $10 in TV production (1 per day @ $10 each) or through DVD production (2 per day @ $5 each).

U.S. AND MEXICO AFTER UNFETTERED TRADE

TV price is $22 each, DVD price is $10 each.

U.S. workers get paid $50 / day.

Mexican workers get paid $22 / day.

Check that these numbers are also consistent with the table, assuming unrestricted trade between the countries. The U.S. workers just make DVDs, and so earn $50 per day. The Mexican workers just make TVs, and so earn $22 per day.

U.S. TV manufacturers can't stay in business under these circumstances; they can only charge $22 per TV (due to "cheap imports" from Mexico) but the U.S. worker can only make 2 TVs per day. So that means the U.S. TV producer could only pay his or her workers $44 / day, yet the DVD producers are offering $50. So no U.S. worker would continue going to the TV factory.

By the same token, the previous Mexican producers of DVDs can't compete with the "overly productive" U.S. workers. Even though DVD prices in Mexico have risen to $10 each, nonetheless the Mexican DVD producer can only pay his workers $20 per day (since each Mexican worker can only make 2 DVDs / day). No Mexican worker would accept that job, since the TV factory is paying $22 / day.

Finally, notice that all workers are richer in real terms than under autarky. The U.S. worker has experienced a reduction in *nominal* wages, but his smaller paycheck can now buy him either 5 DVDs or *more* than 2 TVs. Similarly, the Mexican worker's wages can now buy him either 1 TV or *more* than 2 DVDs.

This makes perfect sense: If the worker in either country wants to spend all of his or her paycheck on the good still produced domestically, then he or she is unaffected by trade. But if the worker wants to buy the product that is now imported, the worker can buy more units than under autarky. That's the whole *point* of trading, after all. You import things from foreigners when this is cheaper than making it yourself.

In summary, make sure you understand the purpose of the example: We are showing that the workers in the United States benefit from free trade with Mexico, even though the Americans' labor is more productive in every line.

The example also shows (though this isn't the crucial point) that some Mexican firms would be unable to compete with American imports, if all trade barriers were removed between the two countries. Many people in discussions of free trade seem to think that the country with cheaper labor has a competitive edge in every industry, but they are mistaken. In our example above, the Mexican firms couldn't compete with American DVD manufacturers, even though Mexican labor costs were lower, because the American workers' productivity more than compensated for the wage differences.

Multiple Choice:
Write the letter of the best answer to each question.

1. An economic philosophy/doctrine which holds that a country grows rich by encouraging exports and discouraging imports.

    A. communism

    B. capitalism

    C. mercantilism

    D. socialism

2. Goods and services sold to foreigners are called

    A   tariffs.

    B. exports.

    C. quotas.

    D. imports.

3. Goods and services bought from foreigners are called

    A. tariffs.

    B. exports.

    C. quotas.

    D. imports.

4. Taxes placed on goods and services bought from foreigners are called

    A. tariffs.

    B. exports.

    C. quotas.

    D. imports.

5. Limits on the total amount people can buy from foreigners are called
    A. tariffs.
    B. exports.
    C. quotas.
    D. imports.

6. Who destroyed the intellectual justification for mercantilist policies?
    A. Thomas Jefferson
    B. Adam Smith
    C. Lord Acton
    D. Thor

7. When applied to trade or trade policies, this adjective suggests modern-day mercantilist sentiment.
    A. strict
    B. obstructionist
    C. deregulated
    D. protectionist

8. Which 1776 book most famously demolished mercantilism as an idea and began to build the case for free trade?
    A. *The Rights of Man*
    B. *The Declaration of Independence*
    C. *The Wealth of Nations*
    D. *Harry Potter and the Laissez-Fairy*

True or False:
Write true if the statement is true or write false if the statement is false.

9. _____ Most economists think that tariffs make trade fair.

10. _____ Trade with Chinese companies benefits American consumers.

11. _____ Free trade only benefits a country if other countries also practice free trade.

12. _____ A government can make its own people (on average) richer by removing trade barriers.

Short Answer:
On the lines provided, answer the questions in 1 to 3 sentences.

13. Could every country successfully implement mercantilism? What about free trade?

_____

_____

_____

_____

_____

_____

_____

_____

_____

14. Explain how tariffs are taxes on domestic citizens, not foreign companies.

_____

_____

_____

_____

_____

_____

_____

_____

_____

15. Explain how penalizing U.S. imports simultaneously penalizes U.S. exports.

_____

_____

_____

_____

_____

_____

_____

_____

_____

_____

Multiple Choice:

1. C   2. B   3. D   4. A

5. C   6. B   7. D   8. C

True or False:

9. F   10. T   11. F   12. T

Short Answer:

13. Could every country successfully implement mercantilism? What about free trade?

SAMPLE FULL CREDIT ANSWER
No, only a few countries could successfully implement mercantilism, because if some countries run trade surpluses, then others have to run deficits. It's impossible for them all to export more than they import, or (what is the same thing) for them all to accumulate more money at the expense of other countries. In contrast, every country can successfully lower trade barriers and enjoy the advantages of free trade.

SAMPLE PARTIAL CREDIT ANSWER
If one country wins at mercantilism, it's only because another country loses.

SAMPLE NO CREDIT ANSWER
With any trade negotiation, there will be winners and losers. Each government must do the best it can for its people.

14. Explain how tariffs are taxes on domestic citizens, not foreign companies.

SAMPLE FULL CREDIT ANSWER
A tariff takes money that citizens want to spend on foreign goods, and diverts some of it to the government. In that sense, a tariff taxes domestic consumers.

SAMPLE PARTIAL CREDIT ANSWER
Tariffs hurt the consumers.

SAMPLE NO CREDIT ANSWER
Foreign companies might get subsidies from their own governments, allowing them to offset tariffs.

15. Explain how penalizing U.S. imports simultaneously penalizes U.S. exports.

SAMPLE FULL CREDIT ANSWER
Ultimately a country pays for its imports with its exports. So if the U.S. government makes it harder for consumers to spend dollars on foreign goods, then foreigners have fewer dollars with which to buy U.S. exports.

SAMPLE PARTIAL CREDIT ANSWER
You buy imports with exports.

SAMPLE NO CREDIT ANSWER
If the U.S. government imposes a tariff, that might help in the short run but then other countries will probably do the same thing.

The Economics of
Drug Prohibition

Drug Prohibition

The material in this chapter may be sensitive for obvious reasons. We have tried to present it in a neutral fashion, without glorifying drug use or otherwise condoning particular practices. However, when contrasting the outcome of a free market in which people voluntarily exchange property titles, versus an interventionist economy where the government coercively overrides property rights, drug prohibition is one of the major vehicles in today's world. It is also an excellent illustration of what is called "the law of unintended consequences," because many of the alleged problems of drug use are actually caused by drug *prohibition*. We emphasize the point that just because something is *legal*, doesn't mean it is ethical or moral. (If someone thinks it would be a bad idea for the government to throw cheating spouses in jail, that doesn't mean the person is "for" marital infidelity.)

Drug Prohibition Corrupts Government Officials

Depending on your policies regarding R-rated movies, you may suggest that the student watch certain films to better understand the scope of corruption even in the U.S. government. For example, *Serpico* (starring Al Pacino) and *American Gangster* (starring Denzel Washington and Russell Crowe) are both excellent films from a cinematographic standpoint, but they also are based on true stories depicting the incredible degree of police corruption necessary for the large-scale drug trade to occur. In order to understand "how the world works," the student ultimately needs to realize just how pervasive drug corruption is among certain American police departments.

The Significance of "Victimless Crimes"

In this section we point out the significance of the government criminalizing activities between consenting parties—often called "victimless crimes." Whether or not the outsider agrees that a mutually beneficial trade is occurring, the fact is that the parties themselves believe it to be so. This fact has consequences, making it much more difficult for the government to stamp out "victimless" crimes as compared to crimes where one party does not consent to the activity. Because "victimless" crimes are commercial transactions, the scope for corruption is much larger than for more traditional crimes. This observation shows that the typical objection to drug legalization arguments—namely, someone who says, "Well I guess we should just legalize murder too, right?"—obscures some important differences between the two classes of crimes.

Corruption as Cause and Consequence

Keep the material in this subsection in mind, when going over the standard supply and demand treatment of drug prohibition. Specifically, when the supply curve (for a good such as heroin or cocaine) shifts to the left after the introduction of stiff legal penalties, the possibility of corruption dampens the move. In other words, producers don't actually say to themselves, "If the price is $1,000 per gram, how many grams of cocaine do I want to sell, knowing that I will spend 20 years in jail?" Rather, the big-time producers say, "If the price is $1,000 per gram, how many grams of cocaine do I want to sell, knowing that I will have to spend such-and-such dollars per week paying off various vice squads and judges, to minimize the chance that I'll spend 20 years in jail?"

Drug Prohibition Fosters Violence

The individual points in this section are self-explanatory. But to step back and give the overall theme: We first note the undeniable connection between drug prohibition and crime; the historical example of alcohol—with its gangland killings during the Prohibition era—makes this clear enough. However, many economic discussions do not really explain *why* prohibition leads to more violence. Worse still, some economists blame the increase in violence on the lack of police protection for drug dealers. (We explain in the text why this is a poor explanation.) In the text, we show that prohibition raises the marginal benefits of violence, and that it lowers the marginal costs. If a government policy raises the benefits and lowers the costs of a particular action, we shouldn't be surprised when people engage in more of it.

Drug Prohibition Reduces Product Safety

In this section we explain how drug prohibition reduces product safety. For example, you may recall the national discussion on the dangers of drug use when promising basketball star Len Bias died in 1986 from a cocaine overdose soon after being drafted to the Boston Celtics. Although the obvious message to kids was, "Don't ever experiment with cocaine!" a less obvious implication was, "When the government tries to keep people safe by banning certain products, the results often backfire." (In other words, using cocaine is more dangerous, when it must be purchased from a black market dealer, as opposed to buying it from a name-brand manufacturer.)

The last example in the student text concerns a hypothetical ban on shrimp. We explain that in the black market for shrimp, there would probably be a shift toward "jumbo" shrimp, relative to the original market outcome. What we have in mind is something like the following: Typically jumbo shrimp sells for a higher price per pound than conventional shrimp. So if the government for some reason placed large penalties on the sale of all shrimp, presumably some entrepreneurs would still sell it, covertly. But because they would have to hide their stash of shrimp in, say, portable coolers filled with ice, the volume they had for storage would be at a premium. Rather than stuffing a cooler full of regular-sized shrimp that had a black market price of $100 per pound, it would be more lucrative for the illegal shrimp dealer to only carry jump shrimp that sold for $150 per pound. In the unregulated market, it doesn't necessarily follow that producers will only carry the type of shrimp commanding the highest price per pound, because it can be profitable to carry both types and simply buy a bigger cooler to store larger quantities of the cheaper (per pound) shrimp. But in a black market where storage space is at a high premium, that option may no longer make sense.

If you can understand the logic of the shrimp example, then you can see why drug dealers would shift to "harder" items in a prohibited market. Going the other way, this analysis suggests that if drugs were legalized, consumers would actually end up consuming "softer" drugs on average, compared to what they currently buy in the heavily regulated market. This is a very important consideration, to the extent that protecting people from their own bad decisions is one of the primary justifications for drug prohibition.

• •

STUDY QUESTIONS

1. What role does economic science play in the analysis of drug prohibition?

Economics cannot say whether drugs should be prohibited or legal, but it can objectively point out some of the (often unforeseen) consequences of drug prohibition. Many of these consequences are blamed on the drugs themselves, when in fact it is the government's prohibition causing or at least exacerbating the problem (gang warfare, drug overdoses, kids becoming drug dealers, etc.).

2. In what sense do cocaine dealers (under drug prohibition) earn hazard pay?

Under prohibition, cocaine dealers operate in a very risky profession. They are at constant risk of going to prison for a very long time, and typically they are more likely to be violently killed than members of other professions. These factors reduce the supply curve of cocaine, driving up the monetary returns until enough producers are willing to tolerate the high risks and operate in the industry.

3. *What is the connection between corruption and a "victimless crime" such as cocaine distribution?

Unlike traditional crimes such as robbery and murder, when it comes to commercial drug transactions there is a customer who wants to give his money to the dealer in exchange for the product. Because there is so much more money involved, and such a huge potential market, illegal drug dealers have the ability to funnel very large bribes to government officials. Also, it is more understandable that police would look the other way when people are consensually breaking laws, as opposed to criminals who are violating the property rights of others through theft or bodily assault.

4. How does drug prohibition raise the marginal benefits of using violence for drug dealers?

The "hazard pay" (see question 2) aspect of illegal drug dealing raises the monetary payoffs to producers. This means that in most cases, a given drug dealer can earn a much larger monetary income (without a corresponding increase in risk of imprisonment, etc.) from expanding his customer base, relative to other industries. Also, the nature of drug trafficking means that there will be many opportunities where the use of violence would allow someone to acquire a suitcase full of cash. These situations don't often arise in other industries, where transactions occur in public view inside buildings.

5. How might drug prohibition contribute to fatal overdoses?

The nature of a prohibited drug industry attracts people who are skilled in police corruption and violence. This is a different type of person from the one who would thrive in a free market. Furthermore, even among the fraction of entrepreneurs who enter the illegal drug industry and are excellent pharmacologists, etc., they cannot earn brand name loyalty as easily as firms in a free market. It is much harder for consumers to seek out and patronize "safe" drug producers in a prohibited market. Finally, the incentives of a prohibited market lead producers and consumers to shift toward "harder" products, increasing the dangers of overdose from consumer error and/or product impurities.

Supplemental Materials

- Mark Thornton, "The Economics of Prohibition," at **http://mises. org/daily/2269**.

  Austrian economist Mark Thornton is an expert on the topic. This article provides a good introduction to his views.

- Walter Block, Channel 6 WDSU debate on drug legalization, video at **http://mises.org/media/1963**.

  This debate features Austrian economist and libertarian theorist Walter Block against an official from the Drug Enforcement Agency. (There is an introductory news feature setting up the context of drug problems in New Orleans, and then the debate begins at the 4:05 mark.) We should point out that strictly speaking, there is no connection between Austrian economics and drug legalization. However, in practice most Austrian economists do favor drug legalization because they also tend to hold libertarian values, and because they see much of the tragedy related to drug use as stemming from prohibition.

- Short film, "The Incredible Bread Machine Film," at **http:// mises.org/MediaPlayer.aspx?Id=4996**.

  This is a half-hour film made by a group of young people in the 1970s. It is something of an underground classic in libertarian circles. It touches on various examples of government interference with citizens' lives, including drug prohibition.

SUGGESTED ACTIVITIES

(1) For students interested in history, you could ask them to explore the origins of the current drug prohibition regime. In other words, it was not always the case in the United States that someone selling cocaine could be sent to prison for decades. (Some proponents of drug legalization point out that hemp was used for commercial purposes in colonial times. They even claim [perhaps apocryphally] that the original U.S. Constitution and U.S. flag were made of hemp.)

(2) If the movie versions would be inappropriate, reading the book *Serpico* by Peter Maas may be an acceptable substitute. The author relays the real-life story of a New York City police officer (Frank Serpico) who refuses to accept "dirty money."

Short Answer:
On the lines provided, answer the questions in 1 to 3 sentences.

1. Contrast drug prohibition with "sin taxes" on liquor and cigarettes.

_____

_____

_____

_____

_____

_____

_____

2. Does it make sense for someone to support drug legalization, while opposing drug use?

_____

_____

_____

_____

_____

_____

_____

_____

3. How might drug prohibition raise the financial marginal benefits of violence for drug dealers? (Hint: This question is NOT asking about the marginal costs of violence.)

_____

_____

_____

_____

_____

_____

_____

_____

_____

4. Define "victimless crime," and list two different examples.

_____

_____

_____

_____

_____

_____

_____

_____

_____

_____

_____

5. Although it is illegal, the drug trade is still a business. Explain.

_____

_____

_____

_____

_____

_____

_____

_____

_____

_____

6. Explain how drug prohibition reduces product safety.

_____

_____

_____

_____

_____

_____

_____

_____

_____

_____

_____

7. Explain this statement: "Most of the problems that people blame on drug use are actually caused by drug *prohibition*."

_____

_____

_____

_____

_____

_____

_____

_____

_____

_____

Short Answer:

1. Contrast drug prohibition with "sin taxes" on liquor and cigarettes.

SAMPLE FULL CREDIT ANSWER
"Sin taxes" are high tax rates on alcohol and cigarettes. Sin taxes are designed partly to raise revenue but also to discourage activity that is frowned upon. However, drinking and smoking are still legal, whereas selling cocaine or heroin is currently a crime that can send you to prison.

SAMPLE PARTIAL CREDIT ANSWER
Sin taxes still allow people to do the activity in question, just at a higher price.

SAMPLE NO CREDIT ANSWER
Citizens are saying that drinking and smoking are sinful.

2. Does it make sense for someone to support drug legalization, while opposing drug use?

SAMPLE FULL CREDIT ANSWER
Yes, because there are plenty of activities (such as cheating on one's spouse) that people think are immoral, yet shouldn't be illegal. Someone might wish that nobody used drugs, while at the same time believing that government efforts to stamp out the practice through incarceration would only make things worse.

SAMPLE PARTIAL CREDIT ANSWER
Yes because you can oppose something without making it a crime.

SAMPLE NO CREDIT ANSWER
No, because if you make something illegal it's obviously because you don't think people should be doing it.

3. How might drug prohibition raise the financial marginal benefits of violence for drug dealers? (Hint: This question is NOT asking about the marginal costs of violence.)

SAMPLE FULL CREDIT ANSWER
By reducing the supply of (illegal) drugs, drug prohibition raises the market price well above the monetary expenses in producing the drugs. That means drug dealers receive a large "markup" for each unit they sell. Therefore, knocking off rival dealers through violence gives cocaine dealers much higher financial benefits than, say, a bookstore would get from blowing up a neighboring bookstore.

SAMPLE PARTIAL CREDIT ANSWER
The street price of drugs is very high so dealers benefit a lot from gaining more market share.

SAMPLE NO CREDIT ANSWER
Drug dealers are already breaking laws so adding murder to the list isn't a big deal. [NOTE: This hypothetical answer is actually pretty good in explaining why drug prohibition lowers the marginal cost of violence, but the question specifically didn't ask about that.]

4. Define "victimless crime," and list two different examples.

SAMPLE FULL CREDIT ANSWER
A victimless crime is one in which all direct parties want the event to occur. Prostitution and cocaine dealing are two examples.

SAMPLE PARTIAL CREDIT ANSWER
A victimless crime has no actual victims.

SAMPLE NO CREDIT ANSWER
A victimless crime is something that doesn't bother anybody.

5. Although it is illegal, the drug trade is still a business. Explain.

SAMPLE FULL CREDIT ANSWER
Drug dealers must produce or buy their merchandise, and sell it to customers in exchange for money. Even though these activities are illegal, they still constitute a (black) market with upward sloping supply curves and downward sloping demand curves.

SAMPLE PARTIAL CREDIT ANSWER
Even though they might be killers, drug dealers still want money.

SAMPLE NO CREDIT ANSWER
We will always have drug dealers because some people are irrational and don't fear long-term consequences like imprisonment.

6. Explain how drug prohibition reduces product safety.

SAMPLE FULL CREDIT ANSWER
Drug prohibition takes away brand name recognition and also gives an incentive for producers and consumers to switch to "harder," more potent drugs than they otherwise would, because these are easier to conceal for a given "fix." Consequently, the drugs are more dangerous than they would be in a free market.

SAMPLE PARTIAL CREDIT ANSWER
Drug prohibition forces people to buy drugs in generic containers from people they will never see again.

SAMPLE NO CREDIT ANSWER
A heroin addict isn't going to check Consumer Reports before getting his next fix.

7. Explain this statement: "Most of the problems that people blame on drug use are actually caused by drug prohibition."

SAMPLE FULL CREDIT ANSWER
The overdoses and crime associated with "drug use" are almost entirely caused by drug prohibition. If drugs were legalized, product safety would improve and consumers would switch to "softer" versions (meaning far fewer overdoses), while gang warfare would disappear. At lower prices, even addicts wouldn't need to steal as much to support their habit.

SAMPLE PARTIAL CREDIT ANSWER
Drug dealers wouldn't kill each other if drugs were legal.

SAMPLE NO CREDIT ANSWER
You ultimately can't force people to be good, they have to choose it on their own.

Inflation

Money Inflation versus Price Inflation

There are some free market enthusiasts who are very particular about the careless use of the term *inflation* and so be sure the student understands the two distinct meanings.

Also note (as we explain in a footnote) that we have deliberately used the term *stock of money* rather than the more familiar *money supply*. Often when people discuss price inflation they will say, "The supply of money rises, and so does the price level." This may confuse the student since we took such pains earlier in the course to distinguish between "supply" (meaning the supply schedule, as represented by the entire supply curve) versus the quantity supplied. In most cases, when people say, "The supply of money rises, pushing up prices," they are not referring to the supply (schedule) of money but rather the actual quantity of money in existence.

We have not included selections from Milton Friedman in the Supplemental Materials because of copyright issues. However, for a well-rounded education in free market economics, the student should be familiar with Friedman's views on money. A very simple introduction to Friedman's overall worldview is *Free to Choose*, whereas a more advanced book is

Capitalism and Freedom. A more technical—though still accessible to the lay reader—book focusing on money is *Money Mischief.* (We should stress that Friedman's views do not necessarily overlap with the presentation of this course.)

There is nothing magical about the particular charts we chose in this chapter; we are simply trying to introduce the student to the various concepts—while warning against common pitfalls—and also warming the student up to working with economic data. As we have stressed throughout this course, basic economic principles do not stand or fall on empirical testing. However, in order to hone one's understanding of the economy (and more narrowly the financial sector), it is necessary to familiarize oneself with various historical patterns. (In the Suggested Activities we explain how to generate these types of graphs yourself.)

Note that the Consumer Price Index (CPI) is maintained by the Bureau of Labor Statistics. They explain the index here: **http://www.bls.gov/cpi/#faq**.

When the media report the latest inflation number, what they are usually referring to is the increase in the seasonally-adjusted Consumer Price Index. (In recent years they have slowly shifted the focus more and more to the "core" CPI, which is the standard CPI with food and energy prices removed. The official justification for this procedure is that food and energy prices are more volatile than some of the other constituents of the CPI, and so by focusing on the "core" analysts can see the underlying trends. However, many cynics think this is simply a government ruse to mask the true increase in prices due to poor monetary policy. After all, consumers think food and energy are rather important parts of their budgets.)

The "pitfall" we are trying to guard against in this section is the erroneous belief that prices follow movements in the stock of money in a mechanical fashion. In other words, some people think that if the number of dollar bills goes up by 20%, then prices rise by 20% (perhaps after a lag). This is wrong for two reasons. First, not all prices rise by the same amount; we know this because *relative* prices bounce around all the time. (For example, the price of a gallon of gas divided by the price of a Big Mac, does not always yield the same ratio.) Second, it's not even true that *on average* prices must rise by the same percentage as the stock of money, even if we adjust for the increase in production of real goods and services. The reason is that the *demand* for money can change as well. Too often proponents of free market economics focus on the supply side of the "money market" while completely ignoring the demand side. But as we know, the market price of something—including the exchange value of units of money—is determined by the interaction of supply and demand.

How Governments Make Prices Rise

Many people find it easier to understand modern currency "debasement" by first learning of the ways in which political rulers used to literally introduce base metals into coins. For a fascinating theory linking the fall of Rome to various government interventions, read Mises's short explanation on pages 761–763 of the Scholar's Edition of *Human Action* (available at **http://mises.org/Books/HumanActionScholars.pdf**).

The Rise of Fiat Money

This subsection provides a short historical background to the topic of government inflation. For more of this history (from an American perspective), see the Rothbard pamphlet in the Supplemental Materials.

The Price of Money Set By Supply and Demand

The important take-away message from this subsection is that the "price" is its purchasing power. In other words, if one

unit of the money good sees its "price" rise, this means that
people must offer more units of goods and services in order to
acquire a unit of money. This is the opposite of how we normally think of money and prices, because we usually quote
prices in terms of money. For example, if the price of a car rises
from $10,000 to $15,000, this actually reflects a falling price of
money. In other words, the purchasing power of money falls,
when the prices of all non-money goods and services go up.
What the average person means by (price) "inflation" is a general rise in the prices of most goods and services. This is the
same thing as saying the general purchasing power of money
has fallen.

At the end of this section we discuss the case of the U.S. in
the mid-1980s, when the stock of money (at least as measured
by the aggregate M1) began rising much more quickly than the
CPI. Again, we are trying to make sure the student realizes that
there are no mechanical formulas in economics; people's subjective valuations ultimately determine the objective prices we
see in the market. For various reasons (probably involving the
sharp income tax rate cuts and the collapse in price inflation
rates) the world demand for U.S. dollar-denominated assets
rose quickly in the mid-1980s, so that the sharp increase in the
money stock did not coincide with large U.S. price inflation.

The Danger of Government Price Inflation

This section spells out the basic reasons that price inflation is dangerous, especially when the price inflation is severe
and erratic. In a subsection we deal with the common retort
that people can protect themselves from government inflation
through various countermeasures and "hedging" strategies. If
necessary, remind the student of the function of money in the
first place, and point out that this function is crippled to the

extent that the purchasing power of money varies in large and unpredictable ways.

The last point of the lesson reminds the student that government spending always diverts resources out of private hands and into politically-directed projects. Therefore, when the government relies on inflation to finance its programs, there is a definite transfer of wealth out of private hands and into government control. This is true, whether or not official price indices show "inflation." In cases like this, what may be happening is that the government inflation is offsetting a *fall* in prices that otherwise would have occurred.

● ●

STUDY QUESTIONS

1. What are the two meanings of the term *inflation*?

Monetary inflation refers to the increase in the amount of money (and possibly the amount of credit), whereas price inflation refers to a general increase in (most) prices.

2. Is there a strict connection between money growth and price increases?

No. All large-scale price inflations have been preceded by a large-scale monetary inflation, but there is no strict formula connecting the two. Especially over short time spans, the two can even move in opposite directions.

3. Why do workers sell their labor hours in exchange for intrinsically useless pieces of fiat money?

People accept money in their exchanges because they expect other people to do the same in the future. (In other words, money has purchasing power *now* because people expect it to have purchasing power in the future.) This can be true even for fiat currency.

4. If the stock of money increases, what happens to the "price of money," other things equal? What does this imply for the prices of goods and services?

As the stock of money increases, the price of money decreases, holding the demand for money constant. But a falling "price of money" translates into rising prices for other goods and services, i.e., price inflation.

5. What is the harm of government price inflation?

Price inflation reduces the effectiveness of a medium of exchange. It becomes more difficult for people to make long-term financial decisions when the market value of the currency itself becomes volatile.

Supplemental Materials

- Henry Hazlitt, *Economics In One Lesson*, Chapter XXIII.

  Hazlitt deploys his characteristically snappy writing to explain inflation.

- Gene Callahan, *Economics for Real People*, Chapter 9.

  Callahan explains the Austrian take on money and (price) inflation. He also refers to mainstream economics (such as the famous "equation of exchange," MV = PT) more than we have done in the student text.

- Murray Rothbard, What Has Government Done to Our Money?, at **http://mises.org/money.asp**.

  This is an entire pamphlet, and the student need not read all of it. However, it is a classic introduction to money, banking, and inflation. The student can also learn more about the gold standard in U.S. history from this pamphlet.

- George Reisman, "The Economics of Inflation," audio at **http://mises.org/media/1001**.

  For those who prefer audio to written materials, Reisman provides a good introduction to this topic. His audience was undergraduates who had an interest in Austrian economics.

SUGGESTED ACTIVITIES

This lesson is a good time to introduce the student to the wealth of data (and easy charting options) at "FRED," a database maintained by the St. Louis Federal Reserve Bank. The URL is: **http://research.stlouisfed.org/fred2/.**

We'll walk you through the re-creation of the chart in the student text. After learning this, you (and the student) should be able to construct your own charts. (Note that this description was written in the fall of 2011. FRED occasionally revamps its website and so the following description may eventually be obsolete.)

The chart in the text shows CPI versus M1. The specific series titles are "CPIAUCNS" (which stands for "Consumer Price Index All Urban Consumer Non-Seasonally adjusted") and "M1NS" (which stands for "M1 Non-Seasonally adjusted"). In order to graph this, we need to first tell FRED which series we want.

From the main FRED page, click on the "Prices" category (which is in a list on the right side of the page). On the next screen click on "Consumer Price Indexes." If you then scroll down, you will see a list of the actual data series. The series we want (i.e., CPIAUCNS) is the second in the list (as of this writing). Click on CPIAUCNS.

Now FRED shows us information about this particular series, as well as the default chart. The dates are not the ones we used in the student text, so we will have to adjust those. But first we'll add the M1 series, then worry about formatting the chart dates.

To add M1NS, click "Edit Graph" which is immediately below the default graph. This brings up a new page. If you scroll down a bit, you will see a green arrow with the option to "Add Data Series." After you click this, a box will appear allowing you to type in a search term. Or, you can click on the "Browse" (to the right of the search box) to look for the next data series you want to add. Go ahead and click "Browse."

When you click "Browse," a new window pops up, showing the list of data categories. M1 is a monetary aggregate, so click "Monetary Aggregates." From the new menu, click "M1 and Components," and then scroll down to find "M1NS." (As of this writing, it is 5th from the top.)

After you click M1NS, FRED should update the chart so that it now shows the entire history of the CPI and M1 series. (Note that CPI goes back to 1913, whereas M1 only starts in the late 1950s.) We now want to trim the dates to match the timeline of the chart in the student text.

Currently "Line 2" of your FRED chart should be "open." (If it isn't, click on the green arrow on the left side of the line, and that should expand the M1 line and allow you to tweak its settings.) One of the options is "Observation Date Range." Change the start date to "1960–01–01." Then click on the green arrow next to the CPI "Line 1," and update the starting date for this series as well.

By clicking the button "Redraw Graph" on the bottom left, you can see the chart with the smaller timeline. However, it still doesn't look the same as the chart in the student text. The problem is that the current graph (on your FRED window) is using different units for the two series. (Specifically, it is showing M1 measured in billions of dollars, whereas it is showing CPI as an index where 100 is the average value of the CPI from 1982 to 1984.) We need to change the units so that both series are graphed as an index, and we want to start them at the same point so that we can observe proportional changes in their levels over time.

For each line (i.e., Line 1 and then Line 2), select the Units pull down menu. Then pick the last option "Index (Scale value to 100 for chosen period)". Finally, type in "1960-01-01" where FRED prompts you to "Or Enter An Observation Date".

After you have done this for both CPI and M1, click "Redraw Graph" and you should now see the same graph (except perhaps for a later ending date) as the one appearing in the student text.

Short Answer:
On the lines provided, answer the questions in 1 to 3 sentences.

1. Explain how the Caesars quite literally debased their currency, and discuss the consequences.

_____

_____

_____

_____

_____

_____

_____

_____

2. If U.S. paper money is really intrinsically worthless, why do people work, steal, and kill for it?

_____

_____

_____

_____

_____

_____

_____

_____

3. Does fiat money have whatever value the government assigns to it?

_____

_____

_____

_____

_____

_____

_____

_____

4. How does a gold standard place a limit on inflation?

_____

_____

_____

_____

_____

_____

_____

_____

_____

_____

_____

5. When prices of most goods and services, measured in dollars, go up, what is happening to the market value of the dollar? Explain.

_____

_____

_____

_____

_____

_____

_____

6. Explain how large and variable price inflation partially defeats the purpose of using money in the first place.

_____

_____

_____

_____

_____

_____

_____

_____

_____

_____

_____

Short Answer:

1. Explain how the Caesars quite literally debased their currency, and discuss the consequences.

SAMPLE FULL CREDIT ANSWER
The Caesars would collect coins containing precious metals (gold and silver), melt them down, add in a "baser" metal to the mix, and then re-coin a larger number, while trying to pass them off as the same coin. Merchants and others adapted by raising their prices (in terms of coins).

SAMPLE PARTIAL CREDIT ANSWER
They inflated the money supply.

SAMPLE NO CREDIT ANSWER
They enacted heavy taxes on the people.

2. If U.S. paper money is really intrinsically worthless, why do people work, steal, and kill for it?

SAMPLE FULL CREDIT ANSWER
U.S. paper money (currently) has an exchange value; people can use it to obtain other goods and services. Because of this, people are willing to work, steal, etc., to obtain U.S. dollars.

SAMPLE PARTIAL CREDIT ANSWER
You can buy things with it.

SAMPLE NO CREDIT ANSWER
It's easier to steal than to work for money.

3. Does fiat money have whatever value the government assigns to it?

SAMPLE FULL CREDIT ANSWER
No. The value or "price" of money is set by supply and demand. The government can use various measures to influence the supply and demand for money, but the government's control isn't absolute.

SAMPLE PARTIAL CREDIT ANSWER
No because the government can't stop inflation.

SAMPLE NO CREDIT ANSWER
Yes, "fiat" means by government command.

4. How does a gold standard place a limit on inflation?

SAMPLE FULL CREDIT ANSWER
Under a genuine gold standard, the government must redeem currency for gold at a fixed conversion rate. If the government is reckless and prints too much paper money, it runs the risk of running out of gold reserves. So a government on a gold standard must exercise restraint in how much currency it creates.

SAMPLE PARTIAL CREDIT ANSWER
Governments can't print gold.

SAMPLE NO CREDIT ANSWER
The statesmen of the late 1800s understood government finance much better, and recognized the folly of runaway inflation.

5. When prices of most goods and services, measured in dollars, go up, what is happening to the market value of the dollar? Explain.

SAMPLE FULL CREDIT ANSWER
The market value of the dollar is dropping, because you need more dollars to buy the same amount of goods and services.

SAMPLE PARTIAL CREDIT ANSWER
Dropping.

SAMPLE NO CREDIT ANSWER
Rising, because the government is printing more money.

6. Explain how large and variable price inflation partially defeats the purpose of using money in the first place.

SAMPLE FULL CREDIT ANSWER

People use money to coordinate complicated exchanges involving multiple people, and they also use it to reduce items to a common denominator. If people aren't confident about the purchasing power of money in the future, they won't be able to plan as well. Because people will try to hold more of their wealth in the form of "real" goods, society will effectively move in the direction of barter.

SAMPLE PARTIAL CREDIT ANSWER

Money isn't as valuable if people don't know how much it will be able to buy.

SAMPLE NO CREDIT ANSWER

No one will want to spend money if inflation is too high.

Government Debt

Government Deficits and Debt

As this is an Advanced Lesson, it pursues certain trains of thought more deeply than the typical chapter in this course. You will have to adjust the difficulty to the student. Of course the most basic point is that government deficit spending leads to higher debt, which entails future interest payments to service the debt.

Interest on the "National Debt"

The purpose of this subsection is to drive home the point that government debt requires interest payments, which can consume a growing portion of tax revenues. In the FINANCING sections, the student can see exactly how the interest payments manifest themselves. Specifically, the government receives a lower amount when it first sells a bond, than when the bond is redeemed the following year. This is why simply rolling over the bonds—in order to keep the outstanding debt level constant—will "lose" money, which is made up for by interest payments out of general tax revenue.

As we explain in a footnote in the student text, in the real world the federal government issues debt of various maturities

(3-month, 6-month, 5-year, etc.). Also, longer-term U.S. government bonds may pay interest through coupon payments, in which case the lender hands over the full face amount in the beginning. For example, if an investor buys a 5-year, $10,000 bond with a coupon rate of 5%, then the investor hands over a full $10,000 upfront to the U.S. Treasury. Then every 6 months the investor "clips a coupon" and gets a $250 payment from the Treasury. (Note that $10,000 x 5% = $500 per year = $250 per 6 months). Then after doing this for 5 years, the investor receives his original principal of $10,000 back. With coupon payments, the investor receives his interest payments separately, and so there is no need to discount the original sum lent to the government.

Government Debt and Inflation

In this section we explain that the popular understanding of government debt and inflation is largely correct, but the underlying mechanism is much subtler than most people realize. We have taken pains to spell out these nuances not so much because the question warrants this much attention, but rather because the discussion provides a good illustration of various principles we have already covered in the course.

If you and/or the student wish to read further on how the Federal Reserve effectively monetizes (some of) the federal government's debt, start with this article from Robert Murphy: **http://mises.org/daily/4029**.

Government Debt and Future Generations

The approach in this section is similar to the previous one. Officially we are exploring the subtle truth of the popular belief that government deficits impoverish future generations—the claim is true, but not for the reasons that most people think. The reason we spend so much time on the issue, however, is that it provides a good reinforcement of the concepts we are trying to teach.

Be sure that the student doesn't take away the wrong lesson from this final section. We point out that government indebtedness goes hand in hand with increased assets (in the form of government bonds) in the possession of the public. Our point here is not to say, "It's a wash, the government debt is no burden because we 'owe it to ourselves.'"

Yes, government debt is a burden, and makes the next generation poorer than it otherwise would be. But the reason it is a burden isn't merely that the government accumulates financial obligations. To prove that this fact per se is not decisive, we brought up the counterbalancing fact of larger private assets (in the form of government bonds). No, future citizens are impoverished because government deficit spending today leads to lower private capital formation, meaning that there are fewer machines, fewer factories, smaller stocks of inventory, etc., for future workers to use. So that's the real reason a government accumulating debt will ultimately make future generations poorer.

The other important lesson is that once we understand exactly why deficit-spending is bad, we see that tax-financed spending is just as bad or even worse. So it is absurd when "deficit hawks" think that the "responsible" thing to do is raise taxes on the current generation, as if that will spare future generations from the consequences of a profligate government.

• •

STUDY QUESTIONS

1. *Explain: "The government deficit is a *flow variable*, while the debt is a *stock variable*."

It only makes sense to measure the deficit in reference to a certain duration of time. For example, we can talk about the deficit during fiscal year 2010, or during the first three months of calendar year 2009. In contrast, the debt is a measure that applies at a particular moment in time. For example, we can talk about the debt as of December 31, 2009. (To understand the flow/variable distinction, an example of water might help. If someone is using a hose to fill a backyard pool, the rate at which the water shoots out of the hose—say, 5 gallons per minute—is a flow variable. On the other hand, the depth of the water in the pool—say, 3 feet—at any given time is a stock variable.)

2. When the government spends more than it collects in tax revenues, what can we say about the budget?

The budget is in deficit.

3. *Is it possible for the government to sell new bonds in a given year, even if the budget is in surplus?

Yes. If the government carries forward an existing debt that is larger than the surplus, then the government ends the period with a debt (though a lower one). If some of the carried debt had to be "rolled over" into new bonds, then the government would have issued new bonds to replace the maturing ones (which were not being paid off with the surplus). For example, in the student text's table, in the year 2012 the government runs a $25 billion surplus, but also (re)issues $75 billion worth of new bonds.

4. Are government budget deficits *directly* inflationary?

No, because by itself a budget deficit doesn't create new money.

5. *Does it help future generations by raising taxes now to close a budget deficit?

No, because the actual mechanisms through which government budget deficits impoverish future generations—lower capital formation, distortions to the future economy when taxes are raised, etc.—are applicable to present tax hikes.

Supplemental Materials

- Robert Murphy, "Government Debt Has No Upside," at **http://mises.org/daily/2006**.

  This essay covers some of the same ground as the student text, but it also deals with two popular notions that the student has probably heard. The first is the view of Alexander Hamilton that a large national debt is good because it gives people an incentive to support the government, and the second is the claim that the national debt is no real burden because "we owe it to ourselves."

SUGGESTED ACTIVITIES

(1) Use the table in the student text as a template, but change the numbers. Leave some of the cells blank and then see if the student can fill them in. For example, you may want to chart out the next three years of the hypothetical scenario in the student text. In the year 2013, you could leave the Interest payment cell blank, because that is already pinned down by the debt level of $75 billion carried forward from the year 2012. (The answer will be $3.75 billion in interest payments in the year 2013.)

(2) Have the student review the history of U.S. federal government budget revenues and expenses to get a sense of the magnitudes (and how they've exploded in recent decades). They are conveniently summarized at the Statistical Abstract here: **http://www.census.gov/ compendia/statab/cats/federal_govt_finances_ employment/federal_budget--receipts_outlays_ and_debt.html**.

Matching:
Write the letter of the correct term beside each concept.

A. Flow variable   B. Stock variable

1. _____ Weight   2. _____ Age   3. _____ Batting average

4. _____ Speed   5. _____ Income   6. _____ Price

Short Answer:
On the lines provided, answer the questions in 1 to 3 sentences.

7. Could a government run a budget surplus while still having a large debt? Explain.

_____

_____

_____

_____

_____

_____

_____

_____

_____

_____

8. If the government retires some of its outstanding bonds during the year, does that mean it's necessarily running a budget surplus? Explain.

_____

_____

_____

_____

_____

_____

_____

_____

9. Explain the accurate sense in which government deficits today make our grandchildren poorer.

_____

_____

_____

_____

_____

_____

_____

_____

_____

_____

Complete the Table.
Fill in the appropriate numbers, using the table in Lesson 22 as a guide. (Assume the annual interest rate on government debt is 5%.)

2010	**2011**	**2012**
Tax Rev: $1 trillion	Tax Rev: $1 trillion	Tax Rev: $1 trillion
Expenditures: $1.2 trillion	Expenditures: $1.3 trillion	Expenditures: $800 billion
Deficit: Q#10	Deficit: Q#13	Surplus: Q#15
Debt at start: $0	Debt at start: $200 billion	Debt at start: Q#16
Debt at end: Q#11	Debt at end: $500 billion	Debt at end: Q#17
EXPENDITURES	**EXPENDITURES**	**EXPENDITURES**
Military: $400 billion	Military: $350 billion	Military: $300 billion
Social: Q#12	Social: Q#14	Social: Q#18
Interest: $0 billion	Interest: $10 billion	Interest: Q#19

Matching:

a. Flow variable   b. Stock variable

1. B   2. B   3. A   4. A   5. A   6. B

Short Answer:

7. Could a government run a budget surplus while still having a large debt? Explain.

SAMPLE FULL CREDIT ANSWER
Yes, because a budget surplus just refers to the government spending less than it collects in taxes, for a given time period (such as a year). The government could do this, while still carrying a large debt that it accumulated from years and years of past deficits.

SAMPLE PARTIAL CREDIT ANSWER
Yes.

SAMPLE NO CREDIT ANSWER
No, because the government uses a surplus to pay off its debt.

8. If the government retires some of its outstanding bonds during the year, does that mean it's necessarily running a budget surplus? Explain.

SAMPLE FULL CREDIT ANSWER
No, because in any given year, some portion of the outstanding bonds will probably mature, meaning the government will have to return the principal to those lenders. Yet the government can

re-enter the bond market and borrow that same principal back again, keeping the outstanding debt at the same level (looking at just these transactions). This process can occur regardless of whether the government happens to be also running a deficit or surplus that year.

SAMPLE PARTIAL CREDIT ANSWER
No, it could be running a deficit and still have to pay off some of the existing bondholders.

SAMPLE NO CREDIT ANSWER
Yes, because to retire a bond means to pay the person off.

9. Explain the accurate sense in which government deficits today make our grandchildren poorer.

SAMPLE FULL CREDIT ANSWER
Deficits today are financed by borrowing money, which drives up interest rates and diverts savings out of the private sector. Other things equal, this reduces the amount of private sector investment, meaning that our grandchildren end up inheriting a smaller collection of machines, tools, and equipment. This reduction in capital goods makes their labor less productive and lowers their standard of living (relative to what they otherwise would have achieved).

SAMPLE PARTIAL CREDIT ANSWER
Government deficits reduce private investment.

SAMPLE NO CREDIT ANSWER
Our grandchildren have to pay for the higher government debt.

Completing the Table.

2010	2011	2012
Tax Rev: $1 trillion	Tax Rev: $1 trillion	Tax Rev: $1 trillion
Expenditures: $1.2 trillion	Expenditures: $1.3 trillion	Expenditures: $800 billion
Deficit: *Q#10* **$200 billion**	Deficit: *Q#13* **$300 billion**	Surplus: *Q#15* **$200 billion**
Debt at start: $0	Debt at start: $200 billion	Debt at start: *Q#16* **$500 billion**
Debt at end: *Q#11* **$200 billion**	Debt at end: $500 billion	Debt at end: *Q#17* **$300 billion**
EXPENDITURES	**EXPENDITURES**	**EXPENDITURES**
Military: $400 billion	Military: $350 billion	Military: $300 billion
Social: *Q#12* **$800 billion**	Social: *Q#14* **$940 billion**	Social: *Q#18* **$475 billion**
Interest: $0 billion	Interest: $10 billion	Interest: *Q#19* **$25 billion**

The Business Cycle

The Business Cycle

T his final chapter is the culmination of the entire course. It draws on several tools developed in previous lessons, and has a very ambitious scope. Without calling it by name, we have laid out the Austrian business cycle theory, or what is also called the Mises-Hayek trade cycle theory. In addition to the Supplemental Materials, for further reading you can try the pamphlet, *The Austrian Theory of the Trade Cycle and Other Essays* available at: **http://mises.org/tradcycl.asp.**

How Governments Cause the Business Cycle

In this section we follow the advice of Friedrich Hayek, who said that in order to understand how things can go wrong in a market, we first need to understand how they could ever go right. What Hayek meant was that it's actually something of a miracle that the economy can generally grow from year to year, with entrepreneurs anticipating customer demands and matching resources to preferences in a smooth way, so that people only notice something is wrong every few years. This is why we first remind the student what we have already studied in previous lessons, concerning sustainable, market-driven growth. (Roger Garrison in his PowerPoint show—discussed in the Supplemental Materials—follows the same pedagogical strategy.)

Sustainable, Market-Driven Economic Growth

The crucial point here is that sustainable economic growth involves a tradeoff, where current consumption drops so that future consumption may increase. This is obvious in the world of Robinson Crusoe, but the same principle applies in a modern economy with millions of people.

Unsustainable, Government-Driven Economic Growth

There is a great deal of information packed into this subsection; you will need to tailor it to the student. The basic story is that when the government artificially lowers the interest rate, it gives the appearance of the prosperity that would accompany a genuine influx of new savings, but this apparent prosperity can't be genuine since it is fueled by nothing more than pieces of paper (fiat money).

For the more advanced student, you can elaborate on the complication that the "illusion" can be quite effective, since everybody really can enjoy an increased standard of living at least for a few years. In other words, during the artificial boom period, the vast majority of workers can get higher paychecks and spend them on real goods and services, and the vast majority of businesses can see a surge in their sales and document great profits on their books. This is all made physically possible because of capital consumption, which is the opposite of (net) investment. In effect, during the artificial boom period people increase their consumption in the present, exploiting a tradeoff of lower consumption in the future.

In a footnote we point out an extremely subtle point, but one which may interest the very advanced student: Technically, it's not correct to say that the economy can finance an increase in output of both consumption and capital goods, by ignoring depreciation. This is because the way the economy deals with depreciation is to produce more capital goods. For example, if a particular entrepreneur engages in maintenance on his factory by buying ball bearings and lubrication oil, and by slowly building up a new machine to replace his current one once it wears out, then these actions are all acts of investment in the creation of new capital goods. So really what happens during the unsustainable boom period, is that entrepreneurs produce the wrong *kinds* of capital goods, and yet they erroneously think that their total output has increased.

The Inevitable Bust Following an Artificial Boom

To illustrate his theory of the boom-bust cycle, Mises would often invoke the analogy of a master builder who is drawing up blueprints for a new house. In order to design the "optimal" house, the builder obviously needs to know how many nails, two-by-fours, workers, etc., are at his disposal. Now if for some reason the master builder thinks he has more bricks to work with than he really does, he will draw up blueprints for a house that are too ambitious.

At some point, the builder would realize his mistake, even if it occurs when he runs out of bricks and yet his blueprints still expect him to use another 1,000 bricks (say) to finish the design. Note that the sooner the builder realizes his mistake— in other words, the sooner he realizes that his blueprints are based on an inflated brick count—the better off he is.

Once the builder realizes his mistake, he will immediately *stop construction of the house.* He will then come up with a revised set of blueprints, which reflect the true number of remaining bricks and other resources. The builder will consider the possibility of "undoing" some of his earlier decisions, but much of the work will be irrevocable. For example, if his workers had cut some boards intending to make a dog house, but now those boards need to be used on the main building itself—to compensate for the fewer number of bricks—this might be an acceptable substitution. But if the workers had already constructed half of the dog house by nailing the boards together and weather treating them, the builder might just have to throw them away. He can't salvage those particular boards anymore, and in light of the brick shortage, the remaining boards are too valuable to use in finishing the dog house.

The analogy with the actual economy should be clear. During the bust period, some firms shut down completely, releasing their workers and other resources to other projects. Other firms continue, but after substituting some of their materials and making other cost-saving adjustments. But from the perspective of the economy as a whole, the various projects are less ambitious than during the boom period, and moreover the post-bust economy is in worse shape *than if the boom had never occurred.* (This is analogous to the fact that the master builder will end up with an inferior house compared to the one he would have designed, had he known the true brick count from the beginning. This is due to the waste of resources during the period when he instructed his workers relying on the faulty blueprints.)

The Causes of Mass Unemployment

Once the student understands the nature of the bust period, the phenomenon of mass unemployment should make intuitive sense. However, you should be aware of two distinct interventions that contribute to widespread unemployment: First, the government/central bank fosters the artificial boom through low interest rates, which inevitably ends up in a bust. So the government/central bank set up a situation in which all of a sudden, perhaps millions of people will be thrown out of work.

However, if that were the end of the story, there wouldn't be a problem of prolonged mass unemployment. Wage rates would start falling and would not stop until the displaced workers had found new jobs.

The reason economies can suffer from very high unemployment rates, for years at a time, is that wage rates (for various reasons) do *not* drop fast enough in order for the labor market to "clear." In terms of a supply and demand framework, the demand for labor has shifted left (due to the change in employers' circumstances and expectations), meaning that the new equilibrium wage is lower. If the actual market wage rate moves downward very sluggishly, then there will be a surplus of labor—also known as "unemployment"—until the actual wage has fallen to the lower equilibrium wage.

There are various government interventions that can slow the restoration of equilibrium in the labor market. One of the most obvious is direct relief payments to unemployed workers, but during the Great Depression (for example) President Herbert Hoover explicitly urged big businesses not to lower their wage rates after the stock market crash of 1929.

For the very advanced student, you might explain that technically, what happens is that there are supply and demand curves for *multiple* labor markets for different types of jobs. The laid-off construction worker, for example, might be used to making $60,000 per year and so he initially refuses to take a job flipping burgers for $20,000 per year. Instead he continues to check the newspaper and place his resume at various websites, hoping for a job that pays at least $40,000. He can afford to do this for months, even though he may have no personal savings, because the government sends him unemployment checks. Strictly speaking, the man is not a "surplus worker" in the fast-food labor market, because (while receiving the government checks) he *wants* to supply 0 hours of labor flipping burgers, at the market wage rate of $20,000 per year.

Now if the government were to suddenly cut off all unemployment checks, our unemployed worker (and many like him) would become much less picky. Several of them might desire a job flipping burgers, which would increase the supply curve of labor in the fast-food industry. This would lower the equilibrium salary, say, to $19,000 per year, making it worthwhile for the employers in the industry to hire the new workers. (In other words the wage rate would need to fall, in order to move outward along the employers' original demand curve for fast-food labor.)

As you can see, the actual mechanics are much more complicated than the simple summary of, "Government unemployment benefits prop up wage demands and therefore slow down the adjustment of the labor market." But if we are going to use just a single supply and demand graph to explain the labor market, then the explanation is good enough for the basic intuition.

• •

STUDY QUESTIONS

1. Why is the business cycle sometimes called the *boom-bust cycle*?

The business "cycle" consists of an upswing period (the boom) and a downswing period (the bust). A chart of GDP or employment might resemble a sine wave, where the peaks corresponded to the height of the boom and the troughs corresponded to the depth of the bust.

2. Explain: "[I]n a sustainable, market-driven expansion—where the interest rate falls because people are consuming less and saving more—the extra resources flowing into the new investment projects are coming from the sectors which are seeing a drop in sales."

A market-driven expansion is sustainable because the increased output of capital goods (which are necessary to allow a higher standard of living in the future) come at the short-term expense of a decreased output of consumer goods. During a market-driven expansion, "total output" doesn't actually go up right away, but only the *composition* of output changes.

3. *Do central banks typically lower interest rates by imposing a price ceiling (analogous to rent control)?

No, central banks do not use penalties and fines to set an artificial price ceiling, as governments do with rent control. On the contrary, central banks lower the actual market rate of interest below its *free-market rate*, by injecting newly created fiat money into the credit market. This moves the supply curve of loanable funds to the right, lowering the "equilibrium" interest rate.

4. *How does capital consumption give the illusion that an economy can have its cake and eat it too?

During a sustainable, market-driven expansion, the capital goods sectors expand while the consumption goods sectors shrink. During an artificial, government-driven expansion, *all* sectors apparently grow. This is the economy "having its cake and eating it too." This apparent paradox is made possible by capital consumption, in which resources devoted to the maintenance of the structure of production get diverted to boost the output of particular capital good and consumption good lines.

5. How does an unsustainable boom lead to mass unemployment?

The boom causes workers to become employed in unsustainable projects. Once the realization sets in, these workers need to be reallocated to other firms or even industries. It takes time for the displaced workers to be reintegrated into the market. (Other government policies can hinder this process.)

Supplemental Materials

- "Fear the Boom and Bust," a Hayek-Keynes Rap Anthem, at **http://www.youtube.com/watch?v=d0nERTFo-Sk**.

  A very popular music video that features a debate of sorts between John Maynard Keynes and Friedrich Hayek.

- Gene Callahan, *Economics for Real People*, Chapter 13.

  Callahan lays out the Austrian business cycle theory in very understandable prose. Some students may find his analogy of a bus easier than Mises's example of a house builder.

- Mario Rizzo, "The Misdirection of Resources and the Current Recession," at **http://mises.org/daily/3348**.

  This is a talk that New York University economics professor Mario Rizzo gave to the Club for Growth / Heritage Foundation in 2009. Rizzo does a good job illustrating that the typical commentary on the "Great Recession" ignored the underlying microeconomics of resource allocation. His discussion is very compatible with our treatment of the business cycle.

- Robert Murphy, "The Mystery of Central Banking," at **http://mises.org/daily/1566**.

  This essay provides yet another analogy or thought experiment to get the student to recognize the superficiality of the common media coverage of the business cycle.

- Robert Murphy, "The Importance of Capital Theory," at **http://mises.org/daily/3155**.

  This essay focuses on the issues of capital consumption and unemployment, using a fanciful story of (Keynesian economist) Paul Krugman being shipwrecked on an island populated by primitive villagers.

- Murray Rothbard, *Man, Economy, and State*, pp. 581–86.

  In this selection, Rothbard develops the idea that in a free market, unemployment is "voluntary" in a certain sense. If you have the student read this selection, be careful to stress that Rothbard is not arguing that, say, a large fraction of the U.S. workforce decided to take an extended vacation during the 1930s. Rather, what Rothbard is showing is that the social problem of unemployment is a creation of the government/central bank. On a truly free market, there wouldn't be widespread "involuntary" unemployment.

- Roger Garrison, "Sustainable and Unsustainable Growth," PowerPoint show at **http://www.auburn.edu/~garriro/ppsus.htm.**

  Garrison's slideshow offers a wonderful illustration of the various interlocking features of a sustainable, market-driven expansion versus an unsustainable, government-driven one. However, Garrison wants mainstream economists to understand the analysis, and so he uses diagrams such as the "Production Possibilities Frontier" that are standard fare in a mainstream textbook. You will have to decide whether it is worth learning the new terminology in order to appreciate the slideshow.

SUGGESTED ACTIVITIES

Discuss the master builder analogy with the student in more depth. Hone in on the point that the longer the builder sticks to the original blueprints, the worse the final house will be. To get this point across, you can work through several examples during the chronology. If the builder realizes the mistake in the very beginning, before the workers even begin digging, then he can revise the blueprints in light of the true brick supply, and the only "waste" will be his own time in drawing up the original blueprints. If the builder realizes the mistake after the first floor is already built, then things are far more serious, because the builder has already gone down a particular path and "locked in" much of the available resources. And if the builder waits until he literally runs out of bricks, then at that point he may have difficulty even sealing off the roof to keep out rain, depending on how erroneous the original brick estimate was.

The important insight is that the builder has more options, the earlier he discovers the mistake; it never hurts to discover the mistake sooner, rather than later. In other words, if the builder realizes his mistake T days into the project, and then revises the blueprints accordingly, the final house can't possibly be better than the one the builder would design if he caught his mistake $T-1$ days into the project. This is because the builder on day $T-1$ is always allowed to mimic his behavior as if the original blueprints were still active. So he can always put himself in the same position as he would have found himself, if he discovered the mistake on day T. That's why the final house will either be the same, and probably much better, if he discovers his mistake sooner rather than later.

Once the student really sees this point, you can ask him or her to evaluate the response of world governments and central banks to the Great Recession following the housing bubble. By engaging in massive stimulus programs, and cutting short-term interest rates to virtually zero, these institutions have done their best to prolong the boom period. They are analogous to outsiders trying to hide the dwindling brick supply from the master builder, who encouraged him not to revise his blueprints, but instead to keep chugging along and keep his workers busy.

Short Answer:
On the lines provided, answer the questions in 1 to 3 sentences.

1. Briefly describe the pattern of a typical boom–bust cycle. (Hint: DON'T explain the causes of the cycle, just explain what the cycle *is*.)

_____

_____

_____

_____

_____

_____

2. What are countercyclical policies? Describe two examples.

_____

_____

_____

_____

_____

_____

_____

_____

_____

3. Why is market-driven economic growth sustainable?

_____

_____

_____

_____

_____

_____

_____

_____

4. Why does the text say that government-driven economic growth can be unsustainable?

_____

_____

_____

_____

_____

_____

_____

_____

_____

_____

_____

5. What is capital consumption? How is it relevant for the theory of boom-bust in the textbook?

_____

_____

_____

_____

_____

_____

_____

_____

_____

6. According to the text, what is the "actual function that a prolonged spell of large-scale unemployment serves," in the wake of a collapsing boom?

_____

_____

_____

_____

_____

_____

_____

_____

_____

_____

_____

ANSWERS — LESSON 23
THE BUSINESS CYCLE

Short Answer:

1. Briefly describe the pattern of a typical boom-bust cycle. (Hint: DON'T explain the causes of the cycle, just explain what the cycle is.)

SAMPLE FULL CREDIT ANSWER
During the boom, most businesses are very profitable and hire more workers. This pushes up wages and salaries, drives down the unemployment rate, and makes households willing to spend freely. Something then changes and causes most businesses to contract, laying off workers and driving up the unemployment rate.

SAMPLE PARTIAL CREDIT ANSWER
The boom seems very prosperous, but then it busts and people get laid off.

SAMPLE NO CREDIT ANSWER
The government causes the boom-bust cycle, not the free market.

2. What are countercyclical policies? Describe two examples.

SAMPLE FULL CREDIT ANSWER
Countercyclical policies are government measures that automatically counteract the boom-bust cycle, at least according to mainstream (Keynesian) economics. An example is the progressive income tax, which pushes people into higher tax brackets during the boom and (allegedly) "cools off" the "overheating" economy. Another example is unemployment insurance, in which the government sends checks to people who are laid off, thereby "propping up aggregate demand" during the bust.

SAMPLE PARTIAL CREDIT ANSWER
They help smooth out the ups and downs of the normal business cycle.

SAMPLE NO CREDIT ANSWER
If the government runs too high a deficit, interest rates will rise and hurt the economy.

3. Why is market-driven economic growth sustainable?

SAMPLE FULL CREDIT ANSWER
Economic growth occurs in the market when households save more, pushing down interest rates, and allowing businesses to invest more. It is sustainable because the households reduce consumption (in order to save more), which frees up workers and other resources to be redeployed into making capital goods rather than consumer goods.

SAMPLE PARTIAL CREDIT ANSWER
It is based on genuine saving.

SAMPLE NO CREDIT ANSWER
It is voluntary.

4. Why does the text say that government-driven economic growth can be unsustainable?

SAMPLE FULL CREDIT ANSWER
If the central bank pushes down interest rates, this can temporarily give the illusion of rapid economic growth. However, it is unsustainable because simply printing up more money doesn't actually create more goods and services. Businesses have started too many projects that cannot physically be completed.

SAMPLE PARTIAL CREDIT ANSWER
It isn't based on genuine saving, it is based on inflation.

SAMPLE NO CREDIT ANSWER
Government doesn't efficiently allocate resources.

5. What is capital consumption? How is it relevant for the theory of boom-bust in the textbook?

SAMPLE FULL CREDIT ANSWER
Capital consumption occurs when the economy isn't producing enough new capital goods, to replace the ones worn out in the

production process. Capital consumption can make the boom period seem prosperous, because people really are enjoying a higher amount of consumption. However, the people don't realize that they are "eating the seedcorn" and are setting themselves up for a drop in their future standard of living.

SAMPLE PARTIAL CREDIT ANSWER

Capital consumption means not producing enough new tools to replace the worn out ones.

SAMPLE NO CREDIT ANSWER

If people become desperate enough during the bust period, they might have to disassemble tractors, factories, etc., and use the spare parts elsewhere.

6. According to the text, what is the "actual function that a prolonged spell of large-scale unemployment serves," in the wake of a collapsing boom?

SAMPLE FULL CREDIT ANSWER

During the boom, workers and other resources were pulled into unsustainable channels. After the collapse, entrepreneurs and workers must figure out how to adapt to the new situation, in light of the harsh realities of the mistakes made during the boom period. There is a genuine search process where people gain information about job openings, available workers, etc.

SAMPLE PARTIAL CREDIT ANSWER

It takes time for workers to figure out the best job they should take, after they get laid off.

SAMPLE NO CREDIT ANSWER

The large-scale unemployment will serve as a lesson to the people who behaved foolishly during the boom years, providing an incentive for them not to be reckless in the future. [NOTE: This hypothetical answer is a decent guess, but the question asks what the text said on the issue.]